# Her Story

A Heartfelt & Hilarious Conversation About Why Beauty
Milestones Should Be Options, Not Expectations.

Heather E. Stark MEDSC

# Contents

Dear Young Heather,
You were always pretty
enough for middle school.

Love,
Older Heather

For Mom and Izzy. Grandmother and granddaughter,
forever bound in the spirit and spine of this book.

"There is no natural body,
but only a cultural body.
The body is a reflection of
the society that presided
over its creation."

Dr. Denis Bruna

# Introduction

Hey, Sweet Girls,

*The first thing I want you and every girl to know is this: You are enough. Your mind, your face, your hair, your body, your legs, your brain, your sense of humor — it's all enough. It always has been, and it always will be. So get a marker and write "I am enough" on a piece of paper. Stick it on your mirror, the wall or, better yet, the ceiling of your bedroom, so it's the last thing you see at night and the first thing you see every morning. Do this for yourself, because you are (without a doubt) enough.*

*I wrote this book because our culture forgets to tell girls they are worthy, intelligent and beautiful. There isn't anything you have to do to earn these things, as they are your birthright. They exist within your spirit, and no one can take them away. Many things and people in this world will trick you into believing that you have no worth or will try to steal it away. However, this is impossible. Sometimes we forget about our worth, but it never goes away.*

*As a former school counselor, I always have been passionate about girls growing up confident and secure in who they are. This passion led me into writing two self-esteem curricula for girls. In working with more than 800 girls, I realized most of them have the same concerns about makeup, puberty, body image and friendships. They tell me there is too much pressure to be fashionable, have flawless makeup, be well-liked, and have the perfect body. This pressure negatively affects the way they feel about themselves. They want to know why this pressure exists and how to "deal" with these expectations.*

*While considered cultural milestones, these things can feel more like obstacles. Each milestone is attached to an expectation that can weigh heavily on a girl's self-esteem. However, no one talks about it. No one talks about why these milestones exist or why girls and women are pressured to fit in and conform. Yet we need to talk about it so that, when it's your time to run this particular obstacle course, you can see the next turn, anticipate the next hurdle, and fully understand your choices. It's part of the story of our lives, which means it's worth a conversation.*

Girls never should feel pressured to conform to a cultural standard. No one has the right to expect you to wear makeup, remove hair from any part of your body, or dress in the latest trends. Whatever you decide is up to you. However, to make the best decisions, you need to understand the history behind these societal expectations. Her Story is a conversation to help you navigate many of the tricky passageways of girl culture without losing pieces of yourself along the way.

The idea for this book came to me as I was hiking one day. (Nature is a great tool for harnessing creativity.) I was preparing to give a workshop about self-esteem, and my mind wandered back to the first time I wore a bra (I share this embarrassing story later in the book). I was very ignorant about bras. I had seen them before, but I didn't understand what they did and why women wore them. My mom never really talked to me about why I needed to wear a bra or how to put one on. So I had to guess what it was for and how to put it on … correctly — a humiliating moment that my mom and I laugh at now.

**The silence surrounding this experience spoke so very loudly to me.**

My mother didn't realize my need for a conversation about bras because she didn't have one with her mom. Chances are, my grandma probably didn't have one with her mom, either. This pattern of silent expectation was established early in history. It's no one's fault. There was a different mindset back then. There were no words to explain bras because, in our history, the expectation for girls to wear one outweighed the need for explaining one. But times have changed. I needed to understand why bras exist, and I bet many of you do too.

When a girl understands the history behind a bra, she realizes it is an option instead of an expectation. The same idea applies to makeup, shaving, fashion, hairstyles and even friendships. We get a say in all of it! The silence between generations of mothers and daughters regarding these long-standing cultural milestones suggests a conversation is overdue.

Our culture has specific ideas of how girls should look, and I never felt like I met those expectations. The pressure to conform made me feel unworthy. Because of my low self-esteem, I made decisions that hurt my mind and body. It took me 30 years to understand that I am enough. My struggles with body image and self-esteem are why I started my business and wrote this book. If we change the conversation about beauty culture, we deconstruct the very things that try to steal a girl's worth. You will grow up with confidence. You have big plans, and I hope they include self-love and appreciation. Knowing and believing in yourself will help you overcome the difficulties you will encounter in life to accomplish your goals. This book will guide you in deciding what is best for you and your body. Of course, if possible, we do need to talk to your parents*. There are parts of this book for them to read. You also can read those parts to understand what they are thinking about and considering. They love you and want the best for you. It's their job to help you make those great choices. Lean on them for support and understanding.

So, let's embark on this journey of self-discovery together! Cheers to loving yourself, understanding most things about beauty culture, and knowing you are enough!

Always,

* Parent refers to any caregiver, whether we're talking about a parent, grandparent, foster caregiver, or other trusted adult.

Please note: This book concentrates on the history of beauty culture in the U.S. Although I briefly discuss the history of some beauty practices in Ancient Egypt, China, Japan, and Europe, I bring it back to the U.S. and explore its impact on the girls and women of today.

# MAKEUP SHAKE-UP

Makeup:

Cosmetics such as mascara or lipstick
to enhance or alter one's appearance.


What I've learned:
Not a necessity for one to be beautiful.

## Chapter I

⁓

## BLUE MASCARA & I DON'T CARE-A
An Honest Confession That I Am Not Clowning Around About

My mother finally let me wear makeup when I was in the seventh grade.
She started me out slowly with blush and neutral lipstick. I was excited
to finally wear makeup like all the other girls. However, the only makeup
I owned was clown makeup from an old Halloween costume. But I didn't let
that stop me. I proudly used red to rouge my cheeks and light brown to color
my eyebrows (like I had seen my aunt do once) and my lips. I was proud of
my matching eyebrows and lips. I thought I looked pretty cool. But, the reality
of this situation was that I did not look cool. I looked like I was wearing
clown makeup — to school!

The following year, Mom permitted me to wear eyeshadow but not liner
or mascara. Still, I snuck-wore those whenever I went to the mall (by the way,
it was 1989 and blue mascara was all the rage). My mother noticed, but let me
continue wearing them anyway. I always appreciated her allowing me to make
those decisions. (The clown makeup? Not so much.)

In ninth grade, I finally could wear liquid foundation and face powder. I had
a problem, though; I didn't know how to choose the right shade of foundation
and powder for my skin tone. I went to the mall with some friends and chose
a shade that I thought would hide my acne. Instead, I chose a shade that was
too orange for my skin tone. I am blonde, green-eyed and, in the winter,
quite pale. I went to school looking like I had painted an orange circle

on my face. The funny thing was, no one mentioned my mistake. NO ONE.
I thought I had nailed the flawless makeup look and went back to school for
a second day with my tangerine face. That weekend, my mother gave me a
much-needed makeover. She showed me how to apply makeup and taught me
how to choose the correct shades of foundation and powder for my skin tone.

In college, I stopped wearing makeup because I didn't want to take the time to
put it on. Sleeping until that very last second before class was more important.
However, after college, when I started working professionally, I started wearing
it again because I thought that's what professional women do — wear makeup.
I never stopped to figure out why I felt that way until after my daughter was
born. When she was 4, she asked to put on some makeup. As I asked her why
she wanted it, I realized I did not know why I liked it. So, I stopped wearing
makeup again until I understood why I started wearing it in the first place.
Nowadays, my makeup practices are best described as "whatever." On any
given day, you will find me with or without makeup. It truly depends on
whether I feel like putting it on.

Wearing makeup is a deeply personal decision for most women. I enjoy
the ritual of putting on makeup. I feel as though it is an act of appreciation.
I want the feeling of glamor when I wear it. I also enjoy being natural when
I do not wear it. This chapter is all about makeup. My goal is to provide you
with all of the information you need to make the best-possible decision for
yourself. You will find some history, notes for your parents, notes for you,
and some fun makeup facts. I hope it will help you decide if makeup is the
right choice for you. Are you ready? Let's begin!

Side note: Several years ago, my mother started taking me on shopping
trips to buy makeup for my birthday. I am not sure why or how this tradition
started; perhaps it was to make amends for allowing me to wear clown makeup
to school. Nevertheless, it has turned into a yearly outing that is more about
spending precious time together and less about buying makeup.

## CHOOSING THE RIGHT SHADE
The Allure of Makeup

Are you considering wearing makeup? The idea of wearing makeup can be very appealing. It can feel very glamorous. Applying eyeshadow and highlighting your cheeks with color can feel luxurious. It's gratifying to get just the right shape to your lips or the perfect flick of the eyeliner right at the outer edge of your eye. Experimenting with different shades of eyeshadow, blush and lipstick is an artistic endeavor. Makeup can be a recreational activity and part of a daily beauty routine.

However, sometimes makeup can feel tedious and encumbering. Once we start wearing it, we can feel trapped into believing we must wear it. Suddenly, our natural faces do not feel beautiful without it. It is sad to hear a woman or girl say she doesn't feel pretty without makeup. It makes me want to push the pause button. It is vitally important for every girl and woman to ask herself, "Why do I wear makeup?"

If the answer to that question is any of these:
• I want to feel confident.
• I want to feel pretty.
• All my friends are doing it.
• It's what girls are supposed to do.
• To cover up my imperfections.

Then I urge you to do some more thinking and research on this subject, because that is not why we should wear makeup. Occasionally, our culture pressures us to make choices based on popularity rather than what is best for us as individuals. We go along with the popular choice because we are worried that someone will make fun of us, judge us, or exclude us. Wearing makeup can feel like a popular, socially acceptable choice.

*Sweet Reader, girls never should make a choice to please someone else. We have to be true to ourselves and do what's best for us. You are so important. I urge you to take time to fully understand the culture you live in because that will help you make the best-informed decisions for your mind, body and spirit. Don't let the world decide for you. You are in charge of you.*

## FIRST APPLY A LITTLE BASE & FOUNDATION
### A Brief History of Makeup in Egypt, China & Europe

Did you know early humans painted their faces for rituals? Both men and women decorated their faces to celebrate religious ceremonies and rites of passage. This is thought to be the earliest use of what we would call "makeup." People in many places worldwide still continue this practice.

In 10,000 BCE (Before the Common Era), Egyptians wore makeup as a sign of good health. They believed makeup pleased the gods and pleased gods would give their protection to the people. Egyptians would wear oils and creams to protect their skin from the sun and to hide body odor. As early as 4,000 BCE, makeup was made by grinding up minerals and other natural ingredients. Then, using wooden applicators, they applied kohl, and a green mineral called malachite around the eyes. Women would use red dye from plants to add color to their cheeks for a healthier appearance and henna to their fingernails for a bit of color (Boyce, n.d.).

In China, women also used plant dye to stain their fingernails. The color of the stain indicated their social class. Women of lower classes could not wear bright colors. But, on the other hand — see what I did there? — Chou dynasty royals wore gold and silver on their nails, while subsequent women of nobility and wealth wore black and red fingernail dye. Pale faces, arched eyebrows, rouged cheeks and dramatic, shapely lips were the preferred makeup trends of the day. Women accented their cheeks for a bit of flair by gluing or drawing dragonfly wings, flowers, or bird feathers on them (Ancient Chinese Makeup, n.d.).

Life in Europe during the Middle Ages was hard, especially in Great Britain. The threat of illness was everywhere, particularly for people living in poverty. Often they lived in close quarters and slept in shared beds. If one family member got sick, the others would too. To further complicate matters, many families could not afford medical help. As a result, people avoided those who appeared unhealthy or had scarring from illness. Both men and women realized that makeup and wigs would hide scarring, sores and hair loss — all indications of a hard life or sickness.

By 1500, France was at the epicenter of the fashion and beauty industry, and pale faces remained the preferred complexion for women (and men). Of course, a tanned face meant you worked outside in the sun. But a pale face indicated wealth. Those with family money didn't have to labor in the sun and could afford to spend their days inside, living a life of luxury.

As time passed, more and more products were made for the face, but not always with the safest ingredients. People were very concerned with their looks but gave little thought to product content. For example, in England, Queen Elizabeth I used white makeup containing lead to hide smallpox scars. Lead is a dangerous chemical that can cause your body to stop absorbing calcium, adversely affecting your kidneys, liver and brain. She reportedly died with a full inch of white lead makeup on her face, which may have caused her death.

Women felt pressure to appear healthy. During this time in history, women didn't have many opportunities for wealth. Their purpose was to marry and to have a family. If a woman looked unhealthy, men might think she wouldn't be good marriage material and too sick to bear children.

By the 1800s, people wanted a clear differentiation between men and women (Option12, 2013). The leaders in European society, church officials and English royalty pressured men to stop wearing makeup so they would appear more masculine. However, England's Queen Victoria took things one step further. She felt makeup was vulgar and impolite. She ruled that the only people who could or should wear makeup were actors appearing on stage. But makeup did not disappear entirely. The desire for a beautiful face is a strong force to be reckoned with, so women continued to use it in minimal amounts.

## Rosy Cheeks
A Brief History of Makeup in the United States of America

Before we go into the history of makeup in the United States, I want you to understand what life was like for a woman living in America (or Europe) during this time. Like I said before, the goal of most women was to marry and to have a family. Women couldn't own land, have a bank account or vote, and very few worked in professions outside the home or attended college. A woman's educational, professional and wealth opportunities were slim. The only commodities a girl had to attract a husband were her body, face, personality and family wealth.

Mothers raised their daughters to become women with impeccable character. Society considered it bad manners for a girl to be concerned with her appearance. It was improper for young ladies to wear makeup. However, society expected them to be beautiful and pleasing to men (which sounds super confusing to me). Proper young ladies were wholesome, well-mannered and charming. A girl's behavior reflected her family and her faith. People noted how a young lady conversed with others. A well-mannered lady listened intently to others and rarely spoke about herself. This mindset continued throughout most of the 19th century. However, several cultural developments forever changed our country's standard of feminine beauty.

These were:
• Indoor Bathrooms
• Department Stores
• Women's Magazines and Hollywood
• World War I
• The Iconic Flapper

At the end of the 19th century, middle- and upper-class homes installed indoor bathrooms instead of using outhouses. These new bathrooms had a toilet and sink with a large mirror. Until this point, families used small handheld mirrors to see themselves. But now, for the first time, girls were seeing their whole faces multiple times a day (and becoming their own worst critics). For girls who had acne, it was upsetting. They became desperate to get rid of this blight on their complexions (Brumberg, 1997).

In the late 1800s, doctors didn't clearly understand why acne developed, much less how to treat it. Both boys and girls had it but, because girls' appearances were supposed to be "pleasing," the threat of acne obscuring their looks became a serious concern. More girls than boys voiced their blemish angst, and acne soon became thought of as a "girl issue." Unfortunately, many acne-prevention products did not work or made the problem worse. In these cases, girls found relief in their ability to cover it up with makeup. Women would create makeup products at home, but the ingredients were typically heavy and greasy. Using these led to more blemishes, which led to more greasy cosmetics to cover it up. It was a vicious cycle. Doctors and pharmacies started working on remedies that would ease a girl's acne-induced anxiety by creating products to clear it up or, at the very least, hide it. It was these pharmacies, doctors and scientists that started many cosmetic companies. They would combine creams, chemicals and other ingredients until they reached their desired goal. Once they had the products, they packaged and sold them to their patients and customers.

In the late 1800s, small stores in urban areas started expanding their departments by adding more kitchenware, bedding or draperies. These stores would buy neighboring properties or move to more significant locations. Over time, these stores became larger, metamorphosing into department stores (Edwards, n.d.). Beauty counters were the perfect fit for department stores.

At beauty counters, women could try different products before buying them. Women loved this concept. By the early 1900s, cosmetic companies were vying for a chance to have their products represented at the counters. The snobbishness against makeup slowly fell away. Women became mesmerized by the glamor of cosmetics that advertised a youthful appearance, acne coverage and beauty. New, powdery products promised women that men would fall in love with their youthful glow.

The outbreak of World War I early in the 20th century brought rapid lifestyle changes for many women. With men off fighting in Europe, they stepped into leadership roles in ways they never had before. As the world saw the positive impact women could make in their communities, they started fighting for equality and slowly gained momentum. Since more women joined the workforce, their daughters had the freedom to go out with girlfriends. Girls influenced each other in ways their mothers hadn't by sharing fashion tips and makeup advice.

Much of this advice came from a rise in women's magazines, which paralleled an upswing in the movie-making industry. These two entities went hand in hand to increase the popularity of makeup. The first movies made were silent films, as there was no way to record sound. As a result, actors had to rely on facial expressions to guide the plot and help the audience understand their thoughts and feelings. However, cameras did not have the clarity that they do today. Using makeup helped the actors convey their feelings to the audience. Makeup accentuated an actor's eyes and mouth, making facial expressions easier to see on camera. Magazines advertised cosmetics that would give women the same look as their favorite women actors (much like today's magazines). Women also could order cosmetics from magazines, which gave those who lived in rural areas a way to purchase makeup.

In 1920, the world met The Flapper. This new fashion trend revolutionized the way women dressed and gave them a new way of being. A flapper was a fashionable young woman intent on enjoying life and having a good time. Until this point, women had to comply with strict social etiquette. But not the flapper; she wanted to be independent and didn't care about the societal expectations of others. The flapper trend shortened women's dresses and hair. It revealed a woman's arms while emphasizing dark, smoky eyes and red lips. Women embraced this daring new trend because it was an exciting form of independence.

The first time the word "makeup" appeared in advertisements was during the 1920s. Before this, products were called by their individual names, but "makeup" was a comprehensive word that meant all the items used on a woman's face. The word came from a Polish American cosmetologist named Maksymilian Faktorowicz who later became known as Max Factor. He produced a line of cosmetic products called "Society Makeup," affordable makeup for women who wanted to look like their favorite movie stars (A History of Cosmetics from Ancient Times, 2016). His makeup company, Max Factor X, remains in existence today.

As we step further into the 1920s, we see women gaining more independence. Not only could most women vote, but they were joining the workforce — which meant they made their own money and had some buying power. Before women earned their own money, they had to rely on the men in their lives to give them some to buy cosmetics. Now that women worked outside the home, they could purchase these items independently. As a result, makeup sales soared with the creation of liquid foundation, powder compacts, powdery blushes and tubed lipstick. These new products gave women more choices to enhance their appearance each day. They also made it easier for women to apply makeup and carry it around in their purses.

I want to take a moment to talk about the story of makeup and women of color. The best thing women can do for each other is honor each other's struggles, stories and victories. We all deserve room at the lunch table, and this book makes no exception.

The world of feminine beauty can be very narrow and excludes many feminine bodies. Women of color did not get representation in the beauty industry until the late 1920s, and even that was minimal. There was an unfounded belief that women of color did not want or need makeup. The harsh, ugly truth was that no one bothered to make cosmetics for them because they were Black and Brown. Companies only made products for White women. So, during the '20s, women of color started creating their businesses to address the lack of products. Many Black women started haircare lines that sold makeup on the side. Unfortunately, no matter how successful these companies were, department stores refused to carry their products. Women of color had to rely on magazine orders and door-to-door saleswomen to get makeup.

In addition, there was deep colorism in the world of cosmetics. Companies would advertise products that lightened the skin, giving the impression that darker skin wasn't beautiful or desirable. This belief hurt many women. It would take several more decades before makeup companies not only made beauty products for women of color but also included them in their advertising (Nittle, 2018).

In the 1950s, makeup companies still were using questionable ingredients. There were regulations covering toys, food, medicine, cars and ovens, but no standards were in place for the products people put on their skin. The government finally realized how unhealthy this was, and Congress created regulations forcing cosmetic companies to use safer ingredients in their products. During this time, we also saw the first TV commercials for makeup. Beauty trends and advertisements continued to entice women to buy and wear makeup to make themselves more attractive. The 1960s brought fun eyeshadow colors, including the classic blue and green hues.

However, it was the 1980s that pushed this bright-color fad to new and daring heights. The '80s invited us to get creative with our makeup choices by giving us dramatic new eyeshadow and mascara colors. Mascara now came in shades of blue, pink and green. Lipsticks strayed from reds and neutrals to an array of colors, from bright oranges to deep purples. Makeup companies encouraged girls and women to be artsy and daring with their makeup choices.

In the 1990s and 2000s, makeup continued to be used to enhance or alter one's appearance. Women could choose neutral colors for a natural look or bright and flashy colors for an intensely bold look. Some men, non-binary, and gender-fluid people have become more comfortable expressing their makeup choices as well. People have grown accustomed to new makeup fads coming and going. Our reactions to radical trends are a bit more tempered, focusing on lotions, creams and other products that protect against acne, sun damage and wrinkles.

Women continue to use makeup to feel young, beautiful and confident. Some girls use it as a recreational activity or as a hobby. They view applying makeup as art instead of a beauty routine one performs before going out in public. You can buy makeup at grocery stores, online, at beauty supply stores, and, of course, in department stores. People get makeup and skincare advice from social media, magazines and the internet. Every day, it feels like a new product on the market promises radical positive change for our faces.

## The Finishing Touches
### Changing the Conversation About Makeup

Throughout history, women had a very narrow role: have a family. They didn't have the same rights as men and had to take power and opportunities where they found them. The beauty industry finally allowed women to own something — to feel beautiful, alter their appearance, and gain a bit of rosy-pink confidence.

It was specifically designed for them at a time when they had little ownership of things. So women took it all in. Women owned makeup. They blindly accepted all that the cosmetic industry gave them without question. They jumped headfirst (so to speak) into beauty trends and helped form society's beauty expectations for the feminine body. While this may have been fun at first, it has boxed women into a narrow definition of beauty. For 200 years, women believed they must wear makeup to look pretty, healthy and attractive. They reacted to makeup exactly as cosmetic companies hoped they would. Women doubted they were beautiful enough on their own, so they bought the powdered promises of a more youthful, prettier appearance.

Makeup can be manipulative. If we do not take the time to understand why we wear makeup, we risk falling into the trap of wearing it to feel pretty and confident. When we wear makeup for those reasons, we feel doubt, shame and inadequacy. If you believe you are pretty only with makeup on, you doubt you are pretty without it. So, before applying that mascara and liquid foundation, we must learn that our faces are enough. Everyone has beauty.

If makeup companies had been honest, they would have told us:
> We saw how society pressured you into pleasing others. We noticed how you treasured youth and understood how much you needed to impress others with your looks. We took it in and saw an opportunity. We invented something that we thought you would like but, to make sure you would like it, we shamed you into purchasing it by instilling fear in you: fear of not being pretty enough or having the right skin color, fear of aging and of not being attractive. We got carried away and enjoyed the money you paid to escape the fear of not being enough. We made you believe the only way to be confident in your beauty was to hide it under makeup.

The truth is, the feminine face is a glamorous masterpiece. It is full of wonder, energy and joy. Your natural beauty is stunning. That eyeshadow never will give you the self-acceptance you desperately seek. That comes from within you. Powders, blushes and lipsticks can bring you smiles, fun looks, and moments of confidence. But, at the end of the day, it all comes off — and we are back to the essence of ourselves, our true faces. The job of makeup is to give you a bit of glamor and a bit of enhancement, but it is in its absence that you will find the true essence of your beauty and finally understand what it means to be genuinely confident.

Makeup is not the culprit. Instead, it's people's expectation behind the products that is shame-inducing.

*Sweet Girls,*
*You are made to look like you. To be beautiful like you — not like a celebrity, not like another girl in class. You were made to be you, and that is enough. You are enough.*

*You are enough.*

*You.*
*Are.*
*Enough.*

*Furthermore, you always will be enough. So do not let anyone decide for you the essence of your true beauty. You get to decide that for yourself. It is your right. Everyone else's opinions must fall to the wayside.*

*There are many delightful ways in which to feel beautiful, and they do not all come from a jar. Being beautiful is about tapping into your spirit and discovering your energy. You do this by engaging in activities that unearth the joy inside of you. When joy and energy mix, they produce confidence. Confidence will bring a distinct look to your being, where your true beauty lies. Makeup never can give you that type of confidence or beauty. It has to come from the joyful energy deep inside of your spirit. You will know when you have found it because it will radiate from within your soul. It will color your cheeks with pink excitement, brighten your eyes with joy, illuminate your smile and give you the glow of happiness.*

*Once you understand these things, you are ready to decide if makeup is right for you. Should you choose to wear it, I hope you have the most fun. Buy all the lipstick and all the eyeshadow in every color. Do this because you hold the key to beauty. You understand makeup has no power over you, so wear it all. You allow it to enhance your natural beauty rather than letting it take your beauty when it fades away. Because, Sweet Girl, makeup always will fade away. It never was meant to be permanent. The wisdom that should come with wearing makeup is knowing that our true and natural beauty remains when it all comes off. Always be excited to return to your natural self.*

*Makeup is nothing but some ingredients a company mixed and sold to us under the guise of it being pretend beauty in a pretty jar. You have true beauty. Those makeup companies need us more than we need them. We can buy from them and have fun with their products, but — instead of our culture and the cosmetic companies telling us we should wear makeup — how about us girls being in charge of how, when and why we wear makeup?*

*Sounds good to me. How about you?*

## The Essence of True Beauty
Things to Ponder Before You Reach for That Lip Gloss

Before you choose to wear makeup:
- Understand why you genuinely want to wear it.
- Understand the importance of skincare before you wear makeup.
  Makeup can clog pores and cause additional acne.
- Understand that the purpose of makeup is not to make you beautiful;
  it is to accent your natural beauty for several hours and then be removed.
- Understand that makeup is a personal choice for all people who want to
  wear it and never make someone feel like they should or should not wear it.
- Understand that you are beautiful without it.
- Understand that wearing makeup is optional all the time. You control
  how much or how little you wear and when you wear it.
- Understand that makeup is not a requirement for dates, work, school,
  get-togethers with friends or other social events.

• Understand that makeup can be the perfect place for bacteria to grow. Resist the urge to share makeup with others.
• Makeup is always optional.

Reasons to wear makeup:
• Because it's fun.
• Because today I want to be adventurous.
• Because today I want to be creative.
• Because today I want to pamper myself.
• Because today I want to spend time appreciating my facial features.
• Because I want to express myself.
• Because I want to.

Parents,

You are a huge factor in helping your daughter decide if makeup is right for her. This topic may bring up strong personal feelings. I remember feeling them as my daughter grew up. When my daughter was 4, I stopped wearing makeup to work for about a year while I figured out why wearing makeup was important to me.

When my daughter turned 13, I told her we could have the makeup conversation whenever she wanted. I also told her, "My opinion is that freshman year is a good year to start wearing makeup; however, please let me know if you have a different opinion." In eighth grade, she said she had a different opinion. My memories instantly returned to when my mother let me wear mascara, so I let her wear mascara. However, she played sports. Sweat and mascara do not pair well together, and she stopped. She started wearing makeup again her sophomore year of high school, but went without during the Coronavirus pandemic. Now, she wears very little makeup but spends about 30 minutes in the morning and evening taking care of her skin. She knows that her wearing or not wearing makeup is none of my business; however, she always can come to me with questions. That being said, I go to her for advice on using a makeup sponge and brushes!

The makeup conversation can be a befuddling one. Go with your gut, using love and grace. If you make a wrong move, apologize, tell her this is new territory for you, and she will understand.

If your daughter is asking to wear makeup, please use the following as talking points for conversation:

• Does she know why she wants to use makeup?

• How does she think makeup will enhance her looks?

• Does she understand that wearing makeup now doesn't mean she will always need/want to wear it?

• Does she understand the importance of skincare?

• How will she remember makeup is fun but not a requirement for beauty or to be confident?

• Mothers may want to think about why they started wearing makeup and why — or why not — it is important to them personally. (However, if you share your opinion with your daughter, please tread carefully and let your daughter make up her own mind.)

• Fathers may want to think about how they feel about makeup and why. (However, just as I told the moms above, if you share your opinion with your daughter, please tread carefully and let your daughter make up her own mind.)

If you are like me and have a daughter and a son, let him hear the makeup conversation between you and your daughter. This way, he will understand why girls may choose to wear or not wear makeup. Bring him in as an ally for his sister and change the conversation about why we wear makeup and our culture's definition of beauty.

## A Little Lip Gloss
10 Fun & Slightly Crazy Facts About Makeup

- In the 15th century, women used leeches to suck their blood so they would have naturally pale faces (Booth, 2019).
- Yearly averages show Americans spend more money on makeup than on education (Zaria, n.d.).
- In ancient Mesopotamia, women used powder from crushed jewels for lipstick.
- Aztecs used crushed, dried beetles to dye their eyes and lips red.
- An odorless alcohol, "ambrein" — obtained from a substance called "ambergris" that is produced in the digestive system of sperm whales — is used by some perfumers to make the scent of perfume last longer.
- A facial originated in China — and still on trend in the States — uses nightingale poop (UV sterilized in modern-day use) for a flawless complexion.
- During the Roman Era, men used lipstick to show their social ranking within the community (Zaria, n.d.).
- The first patented nail polish appeared in 1919. It was light pink.
- During Elizabethan times, women used coal tar for mascara and eyeliner. The tar caused many women to go blind (Nesvig, 2015).
- During her lifetime, the average woman will spend about $15,000 on beauty products (Nesvig, 2015).

## Glitter & Shine
Women Entrepreneurs in the Beauty Industry

### Elizabeth Arden (1884–1966)
Elizabeth Arden's career in the beauty industry started when she was a nurse.

While studying to become a nurse, Arden was curious about how lotions could help burn victims to heal. This interest led her to a job as a beautician's assistant. A few years later, she opened a beauty salon with a partner in New York. After the partnership dissolved, Arden hired chemists and created a line of beauty products named after her, Elizabeth Arden. However, she had a bit of an uphill battle in selling her products. It was the early 1900s, and many people still viewed makeup as vulgar. Elizabeth had to be very careful about how she marketed her makeup line. Her strategy was to make cosmetics socially acceptable. Luckily, the movies were becoming trendier, and cameras showed close-ups of women actors in full makeup. The movie industry not only helped her sell her makeup but also altered society's view of makeup, making it more socially acceptable to wear. Her company survived the Great Depression by bringing in a staggering $4 million.

When Arden passed away in 1966, she had more than 100 salons touting more than 300 beauty products. Her curiosity about lotion turned into a booming business that redefined how people viewed the beauty industry (Biography.com Editors, 2016).

### Eunice W. Johnson (1916-2010)

Eunice Johnson was a problem-solver. When she realized that women of color didn't have the foundation to match their skin tones, she developed a makeup line.

Eunice Johnson was married to John H. Johnson, the founder of the popular magazine *Ebony*. After attending a fashion show in the late 1960s, Johnson observed the Black models mixing foundations to create shades that would match their skin tones because there wasn't makeup in existence for them already. So, Johnson approached several cosmetic companies to ask them to make shades for women of color. When companies denied her requests, she found a private laboratory that agreed to help. Using mixtures from the models at the fashion show, the lab created new foundation shades. Johnson tested the product out on the models, and it was a hit.

In 1973, she opened her line of cosmetics: Fashion Fair. Her line of products eventually expanded to include skin and hair care and fragrances. Many cosmetic companies noted Johnson's success and the need to provide makeup to women of color. They soon started offering a line of cosmetics for darker skin tones. Eunice Johnson's advocacy helped people understand that Black and other women with darker skin deserve as much representation in beauty culture as White women (The Editors of Encyclopedia Britannica, N.D.).

# THE HAIR-REMOVAL RACKET

## Chapter 2

For Best Results, Shave Up the Leg
An Honest Confession About Wild Leg Hair

I was living in England when I first noticed my leg hair. It was an "all of a
sudden" moment for me. One day, while I was sitting in PE, I pulled up one
of my pant legs for one reason or another. Underneath that pant leg was a
shocking mass of confused blonde leg hair. It stuck out every which way. There
was no rhyme or reason to it. Some strands were pointing up, while others were
smashed down. The rest were sticking straight out from my leg as if standing
at attention, paying their respects to puberty.

I don't know why I never noticed it before. We were living in a cold, wet
climate. I rarely wore shorts and, if I was in a dress, I had stockings or tights
on underneath. I quickly pulled my pant leg down and looked around. I was
relieved to see that the girls in shorts had hairy legs too. No one said anything
to me about my crazy, standing-at-attention leg hair. After all, we lived in
England, and hair removal wasn't an expectation for girls. A few days later,
I noticed my friend had hair under her arm. That evening I checked my
own and discovered I, too, had The Pit Hair.

The sudden growth of hair made me uncomfortable. I asked my mom if
I could "shave it off." She said yes. I found her razor and listened carefully
as she told me to lather my legs and armpits with soap (we didn't have shaving
cream) and shave down my leg. (Girls, I love my mother. She is simply the
best, but you don't shave down; you shave up, UP!) I immediately jumped

in the shower, lathered on the soap, and shaved down. Unfortunately, the hair didn't come off; I had just smashed it down slightly. So, I shaved (down) again with a bit more pressure, getting more of the hair — and some skin — off. Finally, it was enough to where I was comfortable showing my legs in PE, Band-Aids and all.

In England, in the mid-'80s, hair removal never came up in conversation between me and any of my friends, as it wasn't a cultural norm. So, I shaved once in sixth grade and then didn't shave again until we moved back to the U.S. the following summer (when I finally learned to shave up).

Back in the United States, I was bombarded with TV and magazine ads that highlighted the beauty of a smooth leg. Although I had spent a big part of my childhood in Europe, I quickly realized that beauty routines differed in America. If I wanted to fit in, I had better play the game. But playing the beauty game takes a toll; you give up a bit of your confidence. However, as I grew into an adult and became more confident in my appearance, I now can admit my shaving game is relatively weak.

Much like makeup, my hair-removal practices are hit and miss. My hair-removal method of choice is shaving, and it's usually because I am going swimming in a pool, wearing a skirt, dress or shorts. I like the feel of air and water on my legs just after a shave. I also like the feeling of smooth skin. But, sometimes, I just don't want to shave. So I don't, and I still wear shorts. I live in a beach town and, if you shave before going into the ocean, it burns a bit. The first time I experienced this phenomenon, I was sure the ocean was filled with acid water. So now, if I am going for a saltwater swim, I keep the hair on my legs and armpits. Hairy is better than burn-y.

When I am not in the ocean, I shave my underarms. I always sweat there when I exercise or get nervous. In my head (regardless of truth), I think that shaving my underarm hair will make the sweat easier to manage. It is my natural preference. As a teen and young adult in the 1990s, I routinely tweezed my eyebrows — which has resulted in a life of barely-there brows. As a woman in her 40s, I occasionally tweeze my eyebrows, but sometimes I just don't have the patience for it and let my eyebrow hairs wander wherever they please. Bottom line: After spending part of my childhood abroad in the '80s, where hair-removal practices weren't the norm, I never would expect a girl or woman to remove hair from her body. After all, hair is natural; hair removal is not.

This chapter is all about hair removal. My goal is to provide you with all of the information you need to make the best decisions possible for yourself. You will find some history, notes for your parents, notes for you, and some fun hair-removal facts. It is all here to help you decide if hair removal is the right choice for you.

Are you ready? Let's begin!

## A Hairy Debate
To Remove or Not to Remove

Body hair is weird. I mean, really. I understand it is necessary. It's supposed to protect us from things like dirt, the cold and the sun, but it still is weird. We go through the first decade of life with some leg and arm hair, not to mention the hair on our heads and our eyebrows and eyelashes. This hair is somewhat manageable. But then, as elementary school ends, our hair grows in ways it didn't before. Our leg hair gets longer, hair grows in our armpits, and other places (we will have to talk about that hair, too — prepare yourself). The awkwardness we might feel is understandable, and so is the impulse to remove unwanted hair.

Some countries have hair-removal expectations, and others do not. In the United States, hair removal is a cultural norm. It doesn't contribute to one's health; it simply is an expectation for girls and women. This assumption usually starts around puberty, when hair grows in places and ways that it didn't before. Boys grow hair on their faces and perhaps their backs and chests. Everyone grows underarm and pubic hair (there, I said it). This sudden growth of hair can feel really embarrassing. For many of us, our first instinct is to get rid of it and act like it never happened. But, after a while, hair removal can start feeling like a chore. Boys get to choose whether to remove hair. However, girls are not always given this same choice. In the U.S., teenage girls and women are expected to have smooth skin. This expectation is unfair. If boys can choose whether to engage in hair removal, why can't girls?

Things get even more confusing when we stop to think that leg and underarm hair is acceptable for boys but not for girls. Female hair removal is an expected and accepted practice. When a girl or woman does not adhere to this expectation, people feel like they can judge her for having hair in places they don't. However, men's hair-removal choices do not incite as much judgment. (That being said, I have witnessed men being judged for either shaving their legs or having hairy backs and chests, but not with the same disdain women face.) Even though body hair is natural, many girls feel embarrassed by it. To have leg, underarm hair or unshaped eyebrows feels wrong and unfeminine. In fact, many girls choose to remove hair simply to avoid embarrassment and judgment.

*Sweet Girls,*

*If you are comfortable with body hair, you shouldn't feel forced to remove it. Sometimes our culture makes us feel pressured to choose based on a cultural norm rather than what is best for us as individuals. We go along with this choice because we worry that someone will make fun of us, judge us or exclude us. Hair removal can feel like a popular, socially acceptable, safe choice.*

*Never feel pressured to make a choice because it will please someone else. We must be true to ourselves and do what's best for us. You are so important to this world, and I urge you to take the time to understand the culture in which you live. These things affect you and the choices you will make in your life. Thinking, talking, asking questions and reading all help us make the best, most informed decisions. Do what is right for your body, mind and spirit. Don't let the world tell you what to do with your body. You are in charge of you. If you choose to remove hair, great. If you decide to keep your hair, great!*

Other reasons to not feel forced into hair removal:

- Other girls do it.
- Bullying.
- So you can wear sleeveless shirts, shorts, skirts or dresses
  (you can wear them without removing hair).
- Swimming.
- Shame.
- Other people's expectations.
- To look older.
- To be attractive.


### First, Exfoliate the Skin
A Brief History of Hair Removal in Egypt & Europe


Men have shaved since 30,000 BCE. Early men used sharp stones or shells to shave or scrape (yikes!) hair off their heads and faces before going into battle. They would do this so the enemy couldn't grab hold of their hair or beard during a fight. The less to grab onto during a battle, the less compromised the warrior (Knight, 2008)! Shaving also helped clean the face of lice, dirt and sweat.

As we fast-forward through time, early Egyptians routinely removed hair as part of a cleanliness regimen. They felt hair was dirty, and shaving or rubbing it off the body became a daily practice. Many wealthy Egyptians rubbed off the hair from their heads and wore wigs instead of having a natural head of hair (Ancient Man and His First Civilizations, n.d.). We see the first "waxing" during Cleopatra's reign. People would place a mixture of sugar, lemon and water on their skin and lay a piece of muslin over the paste. When the paste dried, they would quickly pull off the muslin, and in doing so, it would pull the hair from the body — much like we do today with waxing (The History of Sugaring, 2016).

The Romans had the same inclination toward hair. To be without hair (hair on the head was an exception) was a symbol of youth, beauty and social-class ranking. A man's first shave, which occurred around his 21st birthday, was a rite of passage into adulthood. Wealthier women would remove hair with a pumice stone, razors, creams or even tweezers made from seashells.

In contrast, Greek men grew beards. In fact, it was a crime to remove another man's beard. (I am not sure who would want to remove another man's beard, but it was a crime nonetheless.) A common punishment or form of humiliation was to force a man to shave his beard. Beards were so important that a boy's first beard often was sacrificed to the god Apollo (McKay, 2012). Greek women didn't remove hair to the same extent as their Roman counterparts — in fact, many of them embraced the unibrow.

In England, women removed their eyebrows and hairline along their foreheads. A prominent forehead, or brow, was a sign of beauty. Many paintings of Queen Elizabeth I show her without eyebrows and a spacious forehead. However, it was not customary to remove leg or armpit hair. I am not sure if anyone thought about it, really. After all, women during this time wore clothing that thoroughly covered them. As a result, nobody saw their body hair (Knight, 2008).

## Apply Generous Amounts of Shaving Cream
A Brief History of Shaving in the United States

We will take a slight diversion here as we jump from Elizabethan England to North America in the 1900s. To understand why women started shaving in the U.S., we must first understand the history of the *men's* razor.

Throughout history, many cultures expected men to shave their facial hair. Shaving evolved from sharp stones and shells to knives and then to a sharp knife-like razor, and gradually to a form of the razor we use today. Razors were rough, and men often cut themselves. If a man could afford it, he would go to a barber for a close shave. Barbers were skilled in shaving techniques and knew just the right amount of hand pressure to use so they wouldn't cut a man's face or throat. While this was nice, going to a barber was costly. However, in 1904, an American businessman and inventor named King Gillette had an idea. He created a thin safety blade for replaceable razors that reduced cuts and never needed to be sharpened (Cosmetics and Personal Care Products in the Medicine and Science Collections, n.d.). This razor meant men could shave at home instead of going to the barber. It was a hit. However, men constantly had to buy new razors to replace old ones. Gillette ran ads that encouraged men to be clean-shaven and trim to entice them to continue buying razors.

In the early 1900s, women in the U.S. did not shave. Instead, like their European sisters, American women wore clothing that covered their arms and legs. All of this changed in 1908 when the French clothing designer, Paul Poiret, introduced the world to a fashion craze we had not seen before: a long-limbed woman in a dress that revealed (for the first time) her ankles, part of her calves, and her arms — including her underarm. The dresses were made with lighter material and were vastly different from the heavy, cumbersome dresses of the 1800s. They were more comfortable, and women loved them. But, while women loved the dresses, society did not love the underarm hair that now was entirely on display.

This disdain gave Gillette another idea. He would design a razor for ladies. All he had to do was convince women to use it. He, along with other razor companies, did this by shaming a whole gender. History calls this movement "The Great Underarm Campaign" (Women's Museum of California, 2017). Razor companies started producing magazine advertisements that told women their underarm hair was "unsightly," "embarrassing," and needed to be removed. Soon women's magazines were full of razor ads and other methods for getting rid of "unwanted" hair. Women were told shaving was a sign of cleanliness and true femininity. On the other hand, those with underarm hair were considered unattractive (Women's Museum of California,

2017). Women, always wanting to appear attractive and pleasing, caved to the pressure. Soon, shaving one's underarms was an everyday routine.

By the 1920s, razor companies started targeting leg hair. It was a slow buildup at first. Since it was considered improper for girls and women to show their bare legs in public, women wore nylons or stockings under their dresses. Even though legs were visible under a dress, one's leg hair went unnoticed because of the stockings. Shaving the legs was not as important as shaving under the arms until World War II.

During WWII, there was a ration on many items Americans used. The ration ensured that the government had enough supplies for the American soldiers fighting in Europe, including the nylon used for stockings. Razor companies jumped on the rationing bandwagon and tangled leg hair into their Underarm Campaign, touting it as another embarrassing problem that women needed to eliminate. Razor ads encouraged women to support the war effort by choosing to shave instead of wearing stockings. Women, wanting to do their part, picked up the razor and threw off the nylons. But when the war was over, women went back to wearing nylon stockings — and kept shaving their legs.

The 1960s and '70s brought another fun fashion craze for girls: miniskirts and short shorts. These fads revealed quite a bit of leg. It was another freeing moment for many girls and women, and they wanted to put their best "hairless" leg forward (so to speak). By the mid-'60s, 98% of women in the U.S. shaved (Women's Museum of California, 2017). The wearing of miniskirts and shorts solidified women's silent deal with our culture. Our culture said, "If you are going to show your legs, then you must remove all hair. Deal?" And all of the women whispered, "Deal."

Nowadays, women remove unwanted hair by various methods, including shaving, waxing, tweezing, threading or using lasers. Hair removal is a multi-billion-dollar industry. Most girls grow up knowing that they will remove leg and armpit hair one day. In addition, many will remove some eyebrow hair to attain a beautifully shaped brow. While it is perfectly acceptable to remove hair, it is not okay to expect it.

## DON'T APPLY TOO MUCH PRESSURE TO THE RAZOR
Changing the Conversation About Hair Removal

Removing hair (or not) is up to you. But never feel ashamed for having it. Being shamed into removing our natural body hair means it's time to change the conversation.

If hair-removal companies had been honest, they would have told us:
Feminine hair removal is something we dreamed up to make money. Truth is, your legs and underarms are fine with hair on them; after all, that is how you were made. If guys can have underarm and leg hair, so can you. We saw a money-making opportunity in the hair-removal business, and we went for it. We told you hair in those places was embarrassing and a problem, but it's not. We invented a double standard that people followed and, while we don't mind hair on boys, we want our girls hairless and pretty. You fell into our beauty trap. We fed you advertisements that shamed your body. Then we pretended to create a women's razor (when, really, we just turned the men's razor pink and shaped it a bit differently) and women's shaving cream (which is really just regular shaving cream in a brightly colored can), and we sold them both to you at a higher price than the men's products. We hoped you wouldn't notice, and you didn't …
until now.

*Sweet Girls,*
*You entered the world with hair on your body, and no one has the right to tell you that this needs to change. The only reason people ask you to remove it is that they were taught girls are supposed to remove body hair. To see hairy legs and armpits on a girl goes against what they were taught, which makes them uncomfortable. Girls are not in the business of making other people feel comfortable.*

*You never should feel ashamed about anything on your body. You are enough just the way you are.*
*You are enough.*

*You are enough.*

*You.*
*Are.*
*Enough.*

*Furthermore, you always will be enough. Hair removal will not make you better or prettier. In fact, as soon as you are done removing your hair, it comes back because our bodies are designed to be covered in hair. Bottom line: We get to decide whether we want to remove hair. These are our bodies. We decide if, how, when, where and what we remove or keep.*

## RINSE THOROUGHLY & APPLY A MOISTURIZER
Things to Ponder Before You Remove Your Hair

Before you choose to practice hair removal, ask yourself these questions:
- Why do I want my hair gone?
- Do I feel pressured into removing it?
- Do I understand the different ways to remove it?
- Do I understand that hair removal is not a necessity for being clean?
- Do I know I am beautiful regardless of body hair?
- Do I understand the importance of keeping the razor clean and not sharing razors with others, even my friends? (Razors can carry bacteria that can cause infection.)
- Do I understand I can stop removing hair at any time?
- Have I talked to my parents about hair removal?
- Do I understand that hair removal is optional?

Reasons to Remove Hair:
• Because I like the feel of smooth skin.
• Because I like the look of hairless skin.
• Because I play sports and less hair means less wind or water resistance.
• Because I want to.

Parents,

You are a huge factor in helping your daughter decide whether she wants to remove body hair. The hair-removal topic may bring up strong feelings that you didn't realize existed within you. My daughter started shaving in the fifth grade. One afternoon, she came home from school crying because some girls had made some hurtful remarks about her leg hair. I immediately took her to the store for a pink razor and shaving cream. I had another "all of a sudden" moment at the store. No one should be forced to shame-shave.

I looked at her and said, "Just because some girls made fun of you doesn't mean you need to shave." She said she understood but really wanted to shave. As I reached for the razor, I noticed (for the first time) a difference in prices. The pink razors were more expensive than the blue ones. I always had known that the shaving cream in the pink and purple cans cost more than men's, but I never thought about the razors. What a racket! Razor companies make money from bullying and cultural pressure that they intentionally created. If they hadn't started shaming women for having body hair, I wouldn't be standing in the store with a crying daughter who was embarrassed about her natural leg hair.

Hair removal is a big step, and we want our daughters to be comfortable with their choices. In the end, my girl was the one who initiated the conversation, so I followed her lead. First, I considered her level of responsibility and told her what to do. (Shave up!) Then, I told her I never would expect her to continue shaving. Her hair-removal habits were none of my business. Finally, I made sure she knew to keep her razor and the areas she shaved clean to reduce the risk of infections. By the way, it took her 45 minutes the first time she shaved — ALL THE PATIENCE, PARENTS.

Now for the sensitive part. We have to address pubic hair. Many girls feel shamed by the sight of it while swimming or during sports. However, the skin often becomes irritated in trying to remove it, and red bumps appear, which is equally embarrassing. To remove pubic hair (or not) is a real choice that girls and women feel pressured to make. To avoid it feels like we are inviting a silence around it, making it taboo. I am determined to take the shame and awkwardness away from beauty-culture topics, this one included. In a few chapters, we will talk about period care, which involves the same area of the body. If we don't want our daughters to feel shame about period care, then *why* are we avoiding the subject of pubic hair? Address this subject with your daughter. Be gentle, honest and open. See what her thoughts are before voicing yours. Unfortunately, I didn't have the words to address it with my daughter. I left some silence around this subject on the table, and I shouldn't have. If I had a do-over, I would have said:

Pubic hair is natural. It is awkward because it is right there, covering up our genitalia. Sometimes we feel like we have to remove the part of our pubic hair that isn't covered by our swimsuits or sporting outfits. This isn't a fair expectation because we shouldn't feel embarrassed by it. It is part of us. We all have pubic hair, so pretending we don't is weird. I think we get uncomfortable because pubic hair covers the part of the body that is considered private. You decide how you want to handle that hair. As long as you are doing what is best for you, there is no right or wrong. Whatever you decide, I am here to help guide you through it.

This conversation can be a befuddling one. Go with your gut, love and grace. If you make a wrong move, apologize, tell her this is new territory for you, and she will understand. When helping your daughter through the "to remove or not to remove" process, please consider:

• Why does she want to remove hair?

• Why do you want her to remove hair?

• Why do you not want her to remove hair?

- Does she know the different methods to remove hair?
- Do you know the different methods to remove hair?
- Does she understand hair removal is a cultural choice and not a choice of necessity?
- Do you understand that hair removal is a cultural choice, not necessary?
- Does she understand the importance of keeping hair-removal tools and products sanitary to avoid infections?
- Why do you (parent) remove your hair?
- How do you feel when you see a woman with armpit and leg hair? Why do you feel that way toward her?
- What will you teach your son about hair-removal practices, and does it differ from what you will teach your daughter? Why?
- If you are asking her to wait before she removes hair, why? Is it her age, your comfort level, or do you believe she is not developmentally ready?
- Whether she engages in hair removal, is this a battle you want to engage in?

If you are like me and have a daughter and a son, consider letting your son hear the hair-removal conversation between you and your daughter. Or at least make sure he understands the nuances of feminine hair removal. This way, he will understand why girls may or may not remove hair. Bring him in as an ally for his sister and change the conversation. This conversation may help him decide how he wants to handle his body hair. My son was 11 years old before he realized women grow hair under their arms. Since my daughter and I both shave, he thought it was only guys who grew hair there. I never talked to him about female underarm hair removal until I wrote this book.

## Razor Burn
10 Fun & Slightly Crazy Facts About Hair Removal Throughout History

- King Henry VIII and his daughter, Queen Elizabeth I of England, imposed a special tax on bearded men.

- It wasn't until 1986 that companies started selling shaving cream to women (75 Fun Facts About Shaving, n.d.).
- In her lifetime, the average woman will shave her legs 7,700 times.
- Women and men used to remove hair using a mixture of arsenic (a toxic element found in our earth) and quicklime (a chemical in concrete). When the mixture started to burn, they quickly washed it off, thus removing hair.
- Most girls start shaving between ages 12-14.
- When you shave, you also remove dead skin cells.
- Body hair usually grows out from an individual's skin at a 30- to 60-degree angle (75 Fun Facts About Shaving, n.d.).
- In Elizabethan England, people would remove facial hair by rubbing their foreheads with rags dipped in vinegar and cat poop (Knight, 2008).
- The electric razor was invented in 1930 (Cosmetics and Personal Care Products in the Medicine and Science Collections, n.d.).
- The first shaving cream was used in 3,000 BCE.

## THE PINK RAZOR
Women-Owned Hair-Removal Companies

### Billie

Founder: Georgina Gooley.

Georgina Gooley has turned the shaving industry on its head by promoting body-hair positivity.

The razor company, Billie, operates under the belief that girls and women shouldn't be shamed for body hair, as it is a natural and normal part of being human. Billie launched in 2017. The company promotes body-hair positivity while raising awareness about The Pink Tax (Gooley, 2012). This "tax" is not actually a tax but a cost increase. Some companies that make the same products for both men and women charge more for the products marketed to women (Elliot, 2019). Gooley's company also donates 1% of sales to women's initiatives worldwide. Billie is one of the first woman-owned shaving companies designed specifically for women. Women have been shaving for more than 100 years, and we are just now getting a woman-owned shaving company!

**Fur**
Founders: Lillian Tung & Laura Schubert
Tung and Schubert designed their business to take the taboo away from pubic hair.

Their company, Fur, makes hair-care products that help to soothe sensitive skin while cleansing pores and promoting hygiene. The founders promote hair positivity and support those who do not want to remove their pubic hair by offering products to groom it. They believe destigmatizing this area of hair will help people become less ashamed and more confident in their bodies.

# CRAZY HAIR &
# I DON'T CARE

HAIR:

Any of the fine threadlike strands growing from the
skin of humans, mammals and some other animals.

HAIRSTYLE:

A particular way in which a person's hair is worn.

WHAT I'VE LEARNED:

Not a necessity for one to be beautiful.

## Chapter 3

FEATHERED HAIR & BROKEN WINGS

An Honest Confession of Stubborn Pride Forever Captured in Color Print

My fifth-grade school picture is a pure delight. It tells the story of who I am: part perfectionist, part whatever. It was 1986 or maybe 1987, and feathered hair was all the rage. (Not sure what feathered hair is? Look it up; it's guaranteed to make you giggle.) I coveted this hairstyle. I loved the way it resembled birds' wings. My mother obliged, and off to the salon we went. The stylist trimmed and shaped the sides of my hair. This haircut was going to make me a thing to behold, the envy of all. I remember the stylist taking extra time on the left side of my head. I worried that my hair was not performing in the desired feathered manner. When she was done and I saw the final product, I was, indeed, a thing to behold.

The right side of my hair was winged perfection. However, the left side of my hair was indeed shaped into a wing — a broken one. A nasty cowlick on the left side of my head made my hair just shoot straight out from my head and flap over my ear in a manner that hairspray could not tame. My hair simply would not feather on the left side. No matter what I tried, I had a beautiful wing on one side and a broken one on the other. The right side of my hair was always perfect. The left, a humble reminder that I never would be perfect. Sigh. On the morning of my fifth-grade pictures, I tried so hard to get the left side of my hair to feather, but it wouldn't. So, I changed tactics. Maybe I could get the right side to match the cowlick on the left. I am pretty sure I used half a bottle of mousse that morning. (Never heard of mousse? Look it up;

ît's part hair produĉt, part science experiment.) I went to school with rock-solid, yet slightly crunchy, broken feathers that ĝuck out on both sides of my head. When my friend saw me, she asked if I had fixed my hair like that on purpose. I looked her ĝraight in the eye and lied wîth a quick, "Yes, I like ît."

Truth be told, every single one of us has that one school piĉture from childhood that is soul-crushing. But, as adults, we look back on ît and laugh. Getting that piĉture is a rîte of passage. We all go through an awkward hair ĝage. Unfortunately, there always seems to be a camera around — clicking that awkwardness into permanent memory.

## A Natural Blonde
To Accept Me is to Accept My Hair

If there is one thing moĝ girls and women will tangle wîth every morning, ît's their hair. Forget siblings or parents; hair will bring a girl to tears quicker than ît will make her smile. We have to show up for our hair every day, but I don't think hair feels the same way about us. It seems as though ît has a mind of îts own.

My natural hair color is blonde. I used to get queĝioned about the authenticîty of my hair color a lot. Every Auguĝ, as educators went back to school, I had one coworker who would always say, "Your hair is a lot lighter than I remember" — implying that I highlighted ît during the summer. Every year I would reĝpond, "Yes, my hair usually gets lighter in the summer, wîth all the sun." Then there would be silence. As if she was trying to catch me in a lie. People, hair does get lighter in the sun. Also, even if I did color my hair, ît was no one's business.

When I got pregnant wîth my daughter, a slightly wavy frizz took up residence in my hair. I kinda like the messiness of that look; ît matches my personalîty. My hairĝyle is much like everything else in my life: casual until ît's not. I wear my hair down, in a ponytail, ĝraight, maybe ît gets brushed, maybe not, and then some days I let the wavy frizz take over. There was a time when I dyed it red and another time when it was dark brown. Now there is a natural gray streak on the right side. Sometimes I buy hair color from the store to cover it up. But the color fades rather quickly and the gray always comes back. Truth be told, I don't have the patience to keep up the color. One summer, my son and I dyed the ends of our hair blue. That was fun. Maybe I should try to color the gray part a funky color.

Honestly, I don't know how I feel about gray hair. It's certainly a curious thing. It's a sign of growing older, and that is something Americans find challenging. But I have overcome a lot of hard things in my life, and gray hair is nothing compared to that. So, I will keep my brushed, unbrushed, straight, frizzy, slightly graying hair for now. To me, my hair represents a casual, come-as-you-are attitude. This is who I am. I accept you just as you are; please welcome me just as I am.

In this chapter, we are going to take a closer look at hair, both from historical and cultural perspectives. Although it is not my place to tell the stories of other cultures, I do feel as though I have a responsibility to create space and awareness where there was very little space before. I encourage you to do the same. My goal is to give you perspective on hairstyles. I hope to empower you to wear your hair in a style that best expresses who you are.

Are you ready? Let's begin.

CROWNING GLORY
Learning to Love Your Hair

If the goal of this book is to give the history of feminine beauty culture, then it is only right that this chapter takes a different path than the ones before. Hair represents a lot of things to a lot of different cultures. It is symbolic

of health, wealth, social status, home and personality. We need to change
the conversation on the exclusivity of hairstyles and open our minds to accepting
all hair. Long, short, dreadlocks, mohawks, pink, afros, straight, frizzy, gray,
curly, shaved and bald. All hair gets to be a part of the conversation.
If you feel pressure to:
• Wear your hair in certain ways
• Think people should cover gray hair
• Have long hair
• Buy expensive hair products to smooth out your hair
then we need to change the conversation. Hair is hair is hair. No one has
the right to dictate how your hair should look.

American culture is a mixture of all cultures. Ideals tend to get diluted when
you mix them all together. Carving out space for each culture to honor itself
through hair shows respect and proves that there is enough room for everyone
at the table. Let your hair be natural if you want. Wear it in a hairstyle that
honors who you are or who you want to be. Style your hair the way you are
most comfortable wearing it. Hair and hairstyles deserve dignity and
appreciation. But, above all, create space for one another.

Hair isn't something we really get a choice about. We are born with it and do
the best we can to manage it. Yes, we can color it, curl it, straighten it and cut
it, but hair is stubborn. It eventually will return to its natural state of being,
and this is where we will start our chapter: respecting natural hair and the
styles that represent our familial backgrounds.

If you are wearing your hair a certain way so you can "fit in" with other girls,
then I urge you to stop and think about this: If you knew you always would be
accepted and no one would judge your choices, how would you wear your hair?
If you still would wear it the same way, great. But, if you would change it,
then let's take that feeling, unfold it, and use it as a foundation to build
a conversation on how to embrace your hair.

I am stepping up on my soapbox once again. I know you have heard it before and you will hear it again. I want you to truly understand this point.

*Sweet Reader,*

*Girls never should make a choice because it will please someone else. We have to be true to ourselves and do what's best for us. You are so important. I urge you to take the time to fully understand how things in our beauty culture will affect you. Taking time to understand these things will help you make the best-informed decisions for your mind, body and spirit. Don't let the world make up your mind for you. You are in charge of you.*

## STYLE YOUR HAIR EVERY MORNING
### A Brief History of Hair in Ancient Civilizations

As mentioned before, hair is symbolic of health, vitality, wealth and beauty. To have a head of thick hair, rich in color, makes one the envy of most people. For the ancient Egyptians, Greeks, Romans, Chinese and Japanese, this was a fact of life. Hair was their crowning glory.

Egyptian artifacts depict many of the hairstyles that represent African culture. Roman and Greek travelers describe Egyptian hair as "wooly" or "crisp." Art that characterizes daily life shows people with afro-like hair. Hair tools such as combs found in excavation sites indicate that hair was coarse and needed a tool that could detangle it efficiently. Hair often was worn short or shaved. Shaved hair often was made into wigs (The History and Culture of Black Hair, n.d.).

Boys and girls had bald heads with a single "lock of youth" that grew from the side of their heads (Ancient Egyptian Hair and Beauty, 1990). Hair was worn this way until puberty. After this, boys would keep their hair short, while girls would wear theirs in a ponytail or braids. Egyptian queens such as Cleopatra and Ahmose-Nefertari are depicted with braided hair in drawings and sculptures. Queen Nefertari was buried with braids, and evidence from burial sites indicates that women also weaved extensions into their hair (Ahmose-Nefertari, n.d.) (Astral, n.d.).

Wealthy women decorated their hair or wigs with gold, jewels, linen ribbons and flowers. Hair color was an indication of youth and vitality. When a woman's hair started to turn gray, she would cover it up with wigs or dye from henna plants. The henna dye often resulted in an orange-red color. Working-class women and slaves were forbidden to look like nobility or wear wigs. They often would tie their hair back in a loop or arrange their hair in several braids, worn to the side of the head (Ancient Egyptian Hair And Beauty, n.d.).

In Greece, hair was precious and highly regarded. It often was used as a sacrifice to the gods or shaved as a form of punishment and humiliation. Long hair was favored by both men and women. Women used their hair to display their wealth and status. Their servants or slaves would arrange it in braids, curls and chignons, or loose buns.

The styles were embellished with flowers, ribbons and tiaras. Greek women would experiment with white, gold and red powder to dye hair. Women in the working class often wore their hair in a loose bun at the nape of the neck. Hairstyles in Rome favored those in Greece. Roman women preferred light-colored hair. They typically wore their hair in curls that wound around tiaras or ribbons. Wigs also were popular in Greece and Rome. Unfortunately, they usually were made from the hair of enslaved people.

Somewhere in between the Egyptians, Greeks and Romans, hairdressing became a profession. Hairdressers were highly regarded in their communities and often were paid as much as doctors. In Egypt, barbers often were priests because people believed spirits entered into bodies from the tips of the hair. Therefore, haircuts had to be handled by a religious person (James, 2017).

In Asian cultures, hair rarely was cut. In Ancient China, girls wore their hair in braids or a ponytail until their Hair-Pinning Ceremony. During the ceremony, a girl's hair was washed and elaborately styled. This was a rite of passage that indicated she was ready for marriage (Zhan, 2014).

Married women didn't wear their hair in elaborate styles, as they were not in need of attracting a husband. They also had more practical work to attend to, such as running a household and raising children. They often wore their hair up in a simple bun. Working women would wear their hair in pinned-up braids, as they were not allowed to look like the wealthy (Zhan, 2014). In Japan, hair was worn long. Noblewomen wore elaborate, heavy hairstyles as a symbol of their status. Since they didn't work, they could tolerate wearing these cumbersome styles. Women who worked had simpler styles that didn't interfere with their daily responsibilities (Yabi Writers, 2017).

## Wash Your Hair Twice a Week
A Brief History of Hair From the Middle Ages to the Early 1900s in the United States

As we enter the Middle Ages, the Catholic Church is spreading its power and influence. The church declared the proper length of men's hair and ordered all beards shaved. It also ruled that the hair of married women belonged to their husbands. This meant that it was disrespectful for a married woman to display her hair, so women started covering it. Women grew their hair very long and styled it in braids that wrapped around their heads. Remember the large brow being a symbol of beauty? Women would shave their hairline to widen and accentuate their foreheads. Lice was a huge problem during the Middle Ages and women would spend hours combing out nits (lice eggs).

During the Renaissance, women uncovered their hair but still continued shaving foreheads. This trend was reinforced during Queen Elizabeth I's reign, as she shaved her forehead quite high. She also made red hair an acceptable color. Up until her reign, people associated red hair with witchcraft. However, once Queen Elizabeth I took the throne, women started experimenting with dyes in efforts to create that perfect shade of royalty red (The Hair in the Middle Ages, n.d.). Women wore their hair piled high on top of their heads. This grandiose hairstyle would one day get a queen in some royal trouble!

In France, the hair and makeup of both men and women were nothing short of ostentatious. The Rococo style was a celebration of over-the-top looks and fads. People covered their natural looks in efforts to impress and dazzle others (The Hair of the 18th Century, n.d.).

The French queen, Marie Antoinette, took hair to new heights. Literally. Marie's hairdresser, Léonard Autié, would use padding, wigs, hairpieces and ribbon to create a style called a pouf. He piled her hair into a puffy bun that, at times, would reach four feet in height. Autié also would decorate Marie's hair with trinkets, carefully placing them to convey a message or tell a story about France. As a finishing touch, her hair was powdered with flour. The style took so long to create that Marie would wear it for a whole week without taking it down. As you can imagine, this was not very hygienic. Lice was a serious problem during this time. However, hygienic matters aside, women tried to copy Marie's over-the-top hair. But trouble started brewing.

While Marie and her husband, King Louis XVI, were on the throne, wheat crops in France were failing — resulting in a limited supply of flour that drove up the price of bread and other foods. People were starving and unable to afford life's necessities. Marie's careless use of flour, along with the reckless spending by French aristocrats, angered the citizens of France (Shaw, 2019). Eventually, the French people rose up and overthrew the monarchy. Marie Antoinette's flamboyant fashion and over-the-top hairstyles led people to distrust her. She was found guilty of treason and theft and beheaded for these supposed crimes. After the French Revolution, people returned to more traditional hairstyles.

People looked at wealth with disdain and, because wigs were attributed to wealth, the trend slowly ended.

Hair now was worn pulled back in a bun, giving a nod to Greek and Roman hairstyles of centuries before. Ringlets of hair hung down, framing a woman's face. Hair was seen as a symbol of good character and loving disposition, a reflection of a woman's soul.

Queen Victoria of England felt a natural, pious look was a reflection of good morals. This style and belief traveled across the ocean to America. On Southern plantations and in Northern industrial cities, women wore their hair up, curled, and ribboned. Carefully styled hair was a sign of good breeding, social etiquette and wealth.

Whether it is to cover up the gray signs of aging, try something new or express oneself differently, coloring one's hair has been a sacred practice for many women. Up until the late 1800s, it was an uncomfortable and often painful process that rendered both chemical burns on the scalp and hair loss. In 1863, English chemist William Henry Perkin accidentally stumbled on the chemicals that would change the hair-coloring process forever. While working on a cure for malaria (a sickness found mostly in tropical areas caused by a parasite in mosquitoes that invades red blood cells), he accidentally invented a mauve-colored dye instead. This discovery became the foundation for all hair dyes (Hopp, 2019).

During the 1800s and early 1900s, before Native American tribes were driven into hiding or reservations, one clearly could see how they felt about hair. They believed hair to be a reflection of one's self, an extension of thoughts and identity. It was worn in different styles depending on ceremonies, spiritual rituals or times of mourning. Caring for hair was, and still is, symbolic of how Mother Nature cares for Earth. Children of the culture were taught at a young age how to wash, rinse and brush hair. Helping each other groom brings families closer together (The Significance of Hair in Native American Cultures, 2019). In Indigenous culture, natural hair color is a gift. It is rarely dyed other than for ceremonial purposes. Hair typically is worn long. The act of cutting hair is sacramental and done with great care (Lightening Woman Johnstone, 1998). Many Indigenous people believed and still believe that hair should honor one's self, thereby honoring one's heritage.

## FINGER CURLS, BOUFFANTS & BEEHIVES
A Brief History of Hair From the 1900s to the 2000s in the United States

We have talked about the 1900s and our infamous Flapper before. When she showed up at parties with her short hair styled in finger waves, society went berserk. Many people loved the style and, yet, others were appalled that a woman would cut her hair in such a masculine way. However, the trend caught on, and women flocked to the salons. But the shock of short hair was too much for some women, causing them to faint. Salons stocked up on smelling salts to wake women from their fainting spells. Along with makeup and short dresses, bobbed hair was another symbolic act of freedom for women. Women began deciding for themselves how they wanted to be seen, behave and dress.

In the 1900s, we saw the rise of hairstyles and products for women of color. The fads and fashions of beauty culture long have been based on White women. Women of color were (and at times still are) expected to lay aside their cultures, histories, natural beauty and bodies to adhere to these standards.

How does one keep her culture alive when all she owns is stripped from her, and she is forced to take on the customs, traditions and beliefs of others? For women of color, their hair tells the story of their struggle to maintain an identity while forging a life in America. Efforts to make one's hair less natural and more European date back to ancient Egypt. This pressure was quite evident in the late 1800s with the invention of hot combs. These combs were heated on stoves and used to smooth and straighten hair. The term "good hair" was given to those with European or "White" textures. This term automatically divides and implies other textures are not acceptable (Booker, 2014). Whether the woman was Native American, from South America, Africa or Asia, in many places around the world she was expected to take on the hair-care standards of her White sister … which really doesn't feel very sisterly.

After enslaved people were emancipated, Black people felt pressure to fit into the society around them so they could find work. This also extended to hair. Women felt the pressure to smooth their hair and style it in the same manner as White women. That being said, there were very few products and resources available for women of color. Of the products that were available, many were painful to use and burned the hair and scalps of the women who used them (Jahangir, 2015).

Madame C.J. Walker was the first woman in the United States to become a millionaire. She made her millions by developing a line of hair products for women of color. She even started her own factory, had sales agents, and taught women how to style hair. As time moved on, women of color began to take a stand and embrace their identities by embracing their natural hair. They showed the world their natural textures, their curls and their glamor. Unfortunately, this long-overdue self-expression came at a price.

The 1930s and '40s saw a return to longer, flowing locks. Hair was worn to the shoulders and styled with soft, romantic curls. In the '50s, women let their hair grow to a length that best suited them — although it was rarely worn long. Salon visits were on the rise as women wanted a polished look to their hair. The poodle cut was a popular fad worn by movie stars and the social elite. Hair was cut short and tightly curled. It was a hairstyle that embraced all textures of hair. Hair with more texture also could be styled in an Italian cut. Like the poodle, the Italian was a short cut but hair was worn in a loose, tousled look (Sessions, 2020).

By the end of the '50s, we saw the emergence of the bouffant hairdo or big hair. Hair was curled with large rollers, teased and sprayed, resulting in tall

hair that would hang around for days! The classic ponytail was a popular style
for teen girls during this decade. In truth, the '50s gave women a variety of
hairstyles from which to choose. Whether it was a short pixie cut, French
twist or long soft curls, as long as women and girls were well-groomed,
they could wear whatever hairstyles they liked best.

The '60s followed the trend of women branching out into individual styles.
The signature look of this decade was started by an all-female musical group
called The Ronettes. They took the stage with their hair piled high on their
heads in a shape that best can be described as a beehive. The beehive became
the "it" hairdo. Women flocked to the beauty salons to request the style.

The '60s also were a time of civil unrest in the U.S. People of color were
challenging laws, demanding that they be treated with the same dignity and
respect as White people. Women and men wore their hair in natural curls,
afros, cornrows and dreadlocks. This was a purposeful move away from
"White" hairstyles. Unfortunately, this was met with disdain, as many people
saw it as a threat. Women of color were fired for wearing their hair naturally.
It was seen as an act of rebellion. Can you imagine? People being their natural
selves was seen as a threat to others. Is embracing one's natural self an act
of rebellion?  Hmmm. Let's talk more about that later.

As we moved from the '60s into the '70s, young men and women actively
were moving away from conventional standards of thought and beauty. The
start of the Vietnam War spurred this mindset into a movement. Much like the
flapper of the 1920s, the hippie of the '60s and '70s was a new way of being.
Hippies embraced their natural hair texture and style. It communicated
a readiness to love and accept people for who they were, rather than how
society wanted them to be.

The '80s saw a rise in women entering the workforce. But, as they did, there
was pressure to conform to traditional standards and expectations. If you didn't

conform to workplace standards, you could be fired or miss out on promotions. Hair was cut, curled and styled for the acceptance of others. However, teens still used their hair to express how they felt. The punk-rock look of the '80s, with its mohawks and wild colors, caused many parents grief. Girls were introduced to the crimper that pressed hair into zig-zag waves of fun and big hair was back. Women would curl, tease and spray their hair until it floated about their heads in clouds of blonde, brunette, black and red. Of course, there were the infamous 1980s bangs. Bangs were styled high on the forehead with a curling iron, in a shape that resembled a cauliflower. The creation was then glued in place with copious amounts of hairspray.

The '90s and the grunge scene brought hair back down to basics ... for a while, at least. TV shows had characters who wore their hair in styles that paid respect to cultural roots. The 2000s slowly have opened doors to allow women the freedom to do whatever they want with their hair. We have hair of all colors, wigs, extensions, perms, straighteners and every hair curling and smoothing product on the market. Haircare is an $87 billion global industry (Ridder, 2020). We also are more accepting of religious practices that require girls and women to cover their hair as a sign of modesty.

One hurdle many women are working to overcome is letting their hair naturally fade to gray. For a lot of women, time's natural change of color is a hard part of haircare to accept — perhaps because it is so closely tied to aging. All our lives, we are told to fight wrinkles, put on makeup and stay youthful. To make the conscious decision to "go gray" means forgetting everything society has taught us about beauty. Why does someone else get to tell us how our hair should look? Isn't that the individual's decision? I mean, whose head is the hair connected to?! Why is it so hard to accept and express ourselves as we really are? Is it an act of rebellion to wear our hair how we want it and not as others think it should look? Yes, I believe it is. It is an act of beautiful, rebellious self-acceptance.

## A Hairy Rebellion
Changing the Conversation About Hair

Even though it's your hair, people will have strong opinions about it. Those who choose a style that goes against tradition will encounter the spiciest of judgments. Going against convention is difficult for people to accept. Even I had a hard time when my son said he wanted long hair. People constantly feel the need to tell him to cut it. He had to learn to ignore them. Their opinions are a reflection of narrow beliefs.

The truth is, you have to wear your hair in a manner that best pleases you. Your hair has to be comfortable and manageable for you. That being said, you need to take care of your hair. I know my daughter would get pretty frustrated when I would tell her to brush her hair. Her long hair would get so many tangles in it that wouldn't brush out. Our only choice was to cut it. But she didn't want short hair. She decided to wear her hair back in a ponytail and braid. It worked. Remember, when you commit to a hairstyle, you have to commit all the way. You have to be willing to keep up the grooming, so be sure it is the style you want — not one somebody else wants for you. Of course, the minute you don't want that style anymore, that is fine too. Just be patient as it grows out.

Hair always will return to its natural state. No matter how you cut, style or color it, hair will stubbornly return to itself. It teaches us that no mistake is permanent and we always get another chance. What a relief. We get so many opportunities to express ourselves with our hair. But the first thing we must learn is how to be comfortable with our natural hair before we alter it in any way.

Once we are ready to change things, we must not worry about the opinions of others. Whether it is in a messy ponytail, down, long, short, asymmetrical or pink, our hair is our hair. When someone else instructs you on how you should wear your hair, they are wanting you to commit to their opinions. If you do that, then you also commit to their ideas of upkeep. When we own our hair ideas, we commit to ourselves. Not to society, not to beauty culture, just to ourselves. This is confidence. Just like my stiff, crunchy broken wings in the fifth grade. I owned that hairstyle and rode those broken wings for two whole weeks. After that, I started wearing a headband so I wouldn't have to style them every day.

Hair can be tough. Girl, it can be such a morning deal-breaker. When I let myself worry that it doesn't look right, my day can feel ruined. I have to stop and figure out my thoughts. Who actually cares if my hair doesn't look right? Do I care, or am I worried about what others might think?

*Sweet Girls,*

*Embrace your hair. Let it be an extension of who you are. Take pride in it. If you want it in green curls, short and spiky, or in a ponytail so you don't have to think about it, then so be it. Your hair is yours. Own it. You decide what is best for you and let the opinions of others fall to the wayside. You are not here to make yourself look acceptable to others. You are here to make yourself look acceptable for you and to you. Your hair is whatever you want it to be because it is enough.*

*Sweet girl, you are enough with hair.*
*You are enough without hair.*
*You are enough.*
*You are enough.*

*You.*
*Are.*
*Enough.*

*When styling your hair, remember to:*
*• Style it in a manner that makes you comfortable.*
*• Style it in a manner that best expresses you.*
*• Acknowledge that bad hair days are simply that — one 24-hour period, and not a reflection of who you are.*
*• Understand that your hair is not tied to your beauty.*

• *Bald is beauty.*

• *Learn the greatness of your natural hair before you alter it in any way.*

• *Let others' opinions about your hair be no more than that — their opinions.*

Parents,

Helping your daughter style her hair in the mornings can be a tedious and emotional process. She may have definite ideas about how she wants her hair to look that might conflict with your own. Giving her the freedom to make mistakes will strengthen her resilience, and that breeds confidence. Letting her decide which hairstyle works best for her is a self-esteem builder. Let her be independent in this arena.

Many times I felt my daughter's un-styled hair was a poor reflection on me. Parents, letting our children be independent never is a poor reflection. It is the best thing we can do for our kiddos. Her un-styled hair meant I gave her space to express herself. It meant I was secure in my mothering and told the world my daughter was living by her own standards. Messy hair is nothing more than messy hair. It means only what we assign to it.

When I FINALLY gave my daughter the freedom to wear her hair however she wanted, she learned the value of natural hair. I also ended up buying 1.5 million headbands and ponytail holders. When she was little and wanted bangs, we got her bangs. However, she has puffy, wavy hair. Her bangs were puffy every morning and it drove her crazy. She wouldn't commit to styling her bangs every day so she let them grow out. We had a handful of rough mornings until I bought headbands so she could just push her bangs back and pretend they weren't there. Headbands make things better.

When she wanted short hair, we cut her hair. Without the weight of long hair, her wavy hair sprung into a puffy blonde triangle around her head. She wouldn't commit to smoothing the puffiness every morning and let it grow out. We had one week of rough mornings until she realized she had a choice: She could either dry her hair straight each morning or get used to puffiness. She got used to the puff. Three weeks later, she started wearing a ponytail.

Currently, she wears her hair long. It has been pink, platinum blonde and dark brown. Naturally, it's a deep blonde color and spectacular. She has learned how to tame the puff and make the most out of her waves. To get to this mental and emotional place of hair love, she had to appreciate and learn to work with her natural hair before changing it. If I chose her hairstyles, brushed it all the time or offered my unsolicited opinions, then I took away her independence and self-discovery. Parents, self-discovery is a confidence booster. Those mornings when she was learning to accept her hair were tough. When we bordered on running late, I took over for her, but the next morning I woke her up earlier. Now, she treasures her hair and isn't afraid to experiment with it. Also, I am happy that I don't have to brush out those tangles anymore.

This conversation can be a befuddling one. Go with your gut, love and grace. If you make a wrong move, apologize; tell her this is new territory for you as well. She will understand.

When guiding your daughter with her hair choices:
• Evaluate how you feel about your hair first.
• Think about what traditional standards, if any, you adhere to and why.
• Help her understand the upkeep related to her hair choices.
• Give her space and time to style her own hair (maybe start with the weekends).
• Step in only when she asks (or when time is of the essence).
• Encourage her to verbally express why she likes certain styles (hearing her own words may help her develop confidence in her choices, or she may realize it is not the style for her after all).
• If her style pushes you out of your comfort zone, take time to understand why you feel that way. (What does her hairstyle mean to you and is it fair to ask her to change her mind if it is you who are uncomfortable?)

If you are like me and have a daughter and a son, let him hear the hair conversation between you and your daughter. This way, he will understand why girls may choose to wear or not wear their hair in certain ways. It may even help him decide how to style his hair. Bring him in as an ally for his sister and change the conversation on hair.

Side note: My son wears his hair long. His hair has curls as opposed to his sister's waves. At 10, he didn't care if it was tangled. At 13, he asked his big sister for hair advice and she came through. It was actually a really cool conversation that I proudly eavesdropped on. Hair is hard, but it is harder when we tell our kids how they should wear it.

## Mohawks & Mullets
10 Fun & Slightly Crazy Facts About Hair

- In the early 1900s, women were told if they cut their hair short they would grow a mustache.
- The average person has 100,000 to 150,000 strands of hair.
- Hair is made of keratin. The same substance is found in a horse's mane, hooves and bird beaks.
- Black is the most common hair color.
- Red is the rarest hair color, followed by blonde.
- The average hair has a lifespan of two to seven years.
- When wet, a healthy hair strand can stretch up to 30% of its natural length.
- Split ends can split all the way up to your scalp, giving your hair a thinner look.
- The average person loses 50-100 strands of hair a day.
- Hair starts to regrow about three to four months after it falls out.

## Hair-Care Love
Revolutionary Women in the Hair-Care Business

Annie Malone was one of the first women to emphasize scalp care as part of hair care.

In the late 1800s, Annie Malone, a Black entrepreneur, invented a hair-care product that helped women of color take pride in their hair. Before her product, Wonderful Hair Grower, was created, women used bacon grease, butter, lye or products with an alcohol base to straighten their hair. These items not only left hair greasy and damaged, but they also hurt the scalp. Annie encouraged women to think beyond the hair to the scalp. Beautiful hair was dependent on a healthy scalp. One of her most famous clients was Madame C.J. Walker. Annie helped cure Walker of hair loss by teaching her how to use her products to take care of her scalp. Between her company and more than 30 cosmetology schools, Annie was one of the few women of her time to become a millionaire. When she died, she left a legacy of care not only for hair but for fellow sisters as well (Foussianes, 2020).

Meet Ada Rojas and Aisha Ceballos-Crump, two Latinx women who are revolutionizing the hair-care industry by honoring their heritage and cultural roots.

Ada and Aisha are the founder and co-founder of Botánika Beauty. Their company offers women options to smooth, nourish, protect and spruce up curls. They make their products with natural ingredients found in traditional Latinx communities and stores. These two powerhouses are creating a space that gives Latinx women room to claim their natural hair. Embracing hair and culture in a world that often wants to strip it from you is a revolutionary endeavor. Ada and Aisha are two women daring to care enough about their fellow sisters and change the conversation about Latin hair (Mejia, 2020).

# BRAS & BREASTS,

## AN AWKWARD MESS

BRA:

A garment worn under clothing to support breasts.

WHAT I'VE LEARNED:

While they have their benefits, bras are not a mandate
of feminine fashion or necessary in order to be beautiful.

## Chapter 4

## My First Bra
### An Honest Confession Filled With Wonder, Hammocks, Embarrassment & Resignation

Bras rudely interrupted my life in the fifth grade. I remember finding them on my bed and feeling slightly grossed out and embarrassed by them. I was unaware that my time had come, what bras were supposed to do for me, and how one actually puts on a bra. I was simply aware of the fact that all three bras were USED. That's right; I got hand-me-down bras courtesy of the seventh-grader who lived two houses down. I assumed I was supposed to start wearing them. So, that following day — without talking to my mom — I got up and begrudgingly put on one of the bras. I looked ridiculous. It hung on my shoulders and literally floated around my chest. It did nothing except annoy me.

I was uncomfortable all morning long, but my level of discomfort reached new heights when it came time for recess. At recess, we played tag. It was a cutthroat, boys-versus-girls game of tag. The team that was "it" had to freeze everyone on the other team. So you had better be fast if you were going to avoid getting tagged and be able to unfreeze your teammates. That day, I learned that floating bras prevent you from being fast.

The more I ran, the more friction built up between said bra and my shirt. The bra was slowly riding up until it was entirely around my upper chest — as if I had a uni-boob. Finally, I stopped running and, in all my fifth-grade emotional frustration, I shouted, "TIMES!" I untucked my shirt and reached up underneath it, tugging that bra back down to its rightful floating place. One of my friends saw what I had just done, shrugged her shoulders, and simply said, "Mine does that too." From that brief exchange, I assumed all bras were uncomfortable and, by the end of the week, I had given up on them.

About a year later, I came downstairs dressed for school. My mother took one look at me and said, "Where are those bras?" Frustrated, I stomped back upstairs, dug one out of my underwear drawer, and put it on. This time, it fit better as my breasts had grown a bit and, truth be told, were feeling tender. However, it remained uncomfortable, and I still was confused about why I had to wear it, but not for long. Several days later, I was at a friend's house when she took me outside to show me her family's new hammock. As I watched her get into the hammock, I was hit with an epiphany.

"OOOHHHHHHH … hammocks!" I finally understood the purpose of a bra. Eventually, my breasts will get so big that they would need a hammock of sorts to hold them up. At least, that's what my naïve self thought.

Because I was too embarrassed to ask questions about how bras were supposed to fit, I continued to struggle with them until my 16th birthday. For a birthday present, my mother's three youngest sisters pitched in and bought me bras from Victoria's Secret. I had no idea such a place even existed. I remember opening that box and being awestruck. There was a black bra, a blue bra, and a bra with flowers on it, and there was padding in one bra. These bras also had tags with a number-letter combination. The combination on each tag was "32A." I had no idea what 32 and an A meant when conjoined — but I knew that from here on out, whenever I would buy a bra, it would have the 32A number-letter combination on the tag because 32A bras didn't float or ride up.

My first job in college was at Victoria's Secret. I became a bra expert. I was precious. I learned how to measure women for bras and then taught those women how to measure their daughters for a properly fitting bra. Unfortunately, I also figured out what a 32A meant (small breasts), and

I decided I didn't want to be a 32A. So I learned what a pushup bra with the extra padding was, making me look like a 32C.

However, I needed to make a little more money, so I got a job at a sporting-goods store, where I quickly discovered the ease and convenience of a sports bra. I never had worn a sports bra before, and I was 18 years old. Sports bras were harder to put on, but way cheaper than fancy bras. Although I no longer could pass for a 32C, there were such things as removable bra pads that could give me a boost when needed. I also learned that being a 32A was just fine.

Years and years later, when it came time for my daughter to wear a bra, I was naturally drawn to the sports bra. But, of course, it helped that my daughter asked for the type of bra "you run in and not get fancy in." She grew up wearing sports bras until her 16th birthday, when my younger sister, as a birthday gift, bought her bras from none other than Victoria's Secret. And, when my niece turns 16, I will continue the tradition.

Now, I don't always wear a bra. In the summer, when it's hot (and depending on the shirt I have on), I don't wear one. I am always a bit nervous about this because I worry that I will be judged. There is no other reason I worry about going braless — just that other women will think negatively about me. However, the judgment of others is not reason enough for me to not listen to my inner voice. If I want to go without … then I will go without. It's no one's business.

## The Band Bra

Bra Expectations Are Not "One Size Fits All"

"Puberty" is one of the most awkward words in the English language. I wish there was a less cringey word to describe the stage of development when a preteen body grows into an adult body. However, that's the word we have, so that is the word I will use. Puberty involves hormones that change almost everything about our bodies, make us moody, cause pimples, and result in hair growth in embarrassing places. During this time, two particular milestones happen to a girl. One is biological and the other cultural: her first menstruation cycle and her first bra. This chapter is going to focus on the bra.

A girl's first bra can mark a defining moment in her childhood. It can be exciting, a rite of passage, and/or a moment of maturity. However, it also can be embarrassing, confusing and uncomfortable. While the purpose of a bra is clear — to shape and cover the breasts — whether it actually is needed is still up for debate. It is a perplexing conversation!

Before I go any further, let's just state the obvious. This chapter is going to differ from the others. This one may make you want to roll your eyes, crinkle your nose and avoid the conversation. But, please stick with it; don't stop reading. When we avoid a situation or problem because of discomfort, we let others make choices for us. The status quo becomes the answer everyone accepts because no one challenges it. But, when it comes to our bodies, we have the right to question anything that doesn't make sense. So, we will have to talk about bras and breasts and all that awkward mess.

Parents,

If this chapter causes discomfort or disagreement within you, please keep reading and sincerely think about why you believe girls and women should wear bras. Our daughters are worth hazarding the discomfort of unfolding this conversation. They deserve an explanation about the societal expectation to wear a bra and be told that having the ability to grow breasts is not enough to justify wearing one.

Reasons girls shouldn't feel pressured into wearing a bra:
• Your friends are wearing one
• Being shamed
• Being embarrassed
• Bullying
• Others' expectations

*Sweet Girls,*

*Sometimes our culture makes us feel pressured to choose based on popularity rather than what is best for us. We go along with the popular choice because we are worried that someone will make fun of us, judge us, or leave us out. For example, wearing a bra is something almost every girl in the U.S. does without considering whether she needs it or wants it. It is almost automatic, and that is not okay.*

*You never should make a choice simply because it will please someone else. We have to be true to ourselves and do what's best for us. You are so important to this world, and I urge you to take the time to fully understand the world and culture in which you live. These things affect you and the choices you will make with your life. Thinking, talking, asking questions and reading helps us make the best, most informed decisions. You must do what is right for your body, mind and spirit. Don't let the world tell you what to do with your body. You are in charge of you.*

*This chapter will help you understand why bras are a part of our culture. It will give a brief history of bras and why women started wearing them. After reading, I hope you will understand how wearing a bra came to be part of our cultural expectations and then fully decide if bras are the right choice for you.*

*Are you ready? Let's begin!*

## WHALEBONE & OTHER BINDINGS
### All Hail the Royal Corset, the Bra's Predecessor

The first bras have been traced back to early Roman civilizations. There is an ancient mosaic mural called "Bikini Girls." The picture shows women playing sports while wearing strapless bands across their chests (Michalska, 2017). It's unclear if the women are wearing the bands to cover themselves in the name of modesty or to bind their chests while playing sports. However, historians believe this is one of the earliest pieces of evidence showing women wearing bras. This also gives us a perfect segue to dive deep into understanding the history of bras.

In ancient Rome, fashion trends favored small chests. Evidence shows women wrapped material around their chests to bind the breasts for this effect. However, the first bra did not appear until hundreds of years later. But, somewhere between the binding of ancient Rome and the American bra, the infamous corset entered the picture.

The corset made its fashion debut in Italy during the 16th century and took the world by storm! A noblewoman named Catherine de Medici brought it to France, and people went crazy for it. The corset is a close-fitting undergarment that fits around the torso by design. It is made with stiffened or sturdy material and reinforced with long, thin pieces of whalebone — or, in later years, metal — vertically inserted into the layers of fabric. It was tightened by pulling laces located either on the front or back of the corset. This garment made the waist appear smaller, the stomach flatter, and lifted the breasts (Corset History, n.d).

When the corset first appeared on the market, both men and women wore it. By the mid-1800s, men stopped wearing them, but women continued. A side benefit to the corset was that it helped a woman stand up straight and bear the weight of her heavy dresses. This was important, because perfect posture was a sign of beauty and gentility.

Women would squeeze themselves into tiny corsets. The most coveted silhouette was a small waist and wide hips. To achieve this, women (and girls) would pull their corsets so tight that breathing became difficult and lack of oxygen caused them to faint. In fact, corsets were so restrictive that many women couldn't even sit in chairs!

During the 18th and 19th centuries, doctors started voicing concerns over the garment. They discovered that, over time, the tight fit caused breathing difficulties as it pushed and squeezed many of the organs within the torso out of place. In addition, after repeated use, it could change the structure of the rib cage.

Another danger was that women often wore corsets during pregnancy. This endangered the life of their unborn children and made childbirth difficult. Yet, despite warnings, women — feeling the unrelenting pressure to appear fashionable and beautiful — continued to tighten their corsets. As a result, the corset remained at the forefront of feminine fashion until the 1900s.

## RIBBONS & HANDKERCHIEFS
A Brief History of Bras in the United States

In the early 1900s, women were introduced to a fashion trend they never had seen before: a lightweight dress revealing a woman's arms and ankles that hung loosely on the body. Around this same time, Mary Phelps Jacob, a New York socialite, had a small fashion revelation of her own.

Mary planned to attend a party but had a problem: her new dress did not accommodate her corset. The corset peeked out from under it since it was loose-fitting at the top. Mary couldn't wear her new dress with the corset peeking through, but she also needed to cover her breasts. So, in a moment of inspiration, Mary and her maids stitched together two handkerchiefs with some ribbon. Her hanky creation worked perfectly. It covered the chest and freed her from the corset (Nhean, 2016).

Mary's friends fell in love with her new "brassiere" and wanted one for themselves. She tried to make a viable business selling her latest creation. However, she could not make it profitable and sold the brassiere rights to a corset company. Mary's bra changed the world of women's fashion. Society once had deemed corsets the proper garment to support the breasts. But now, society was open to the possibility of something smaller and more comfortable.

World War I reinforced this new mindset. When the war started, corsets were made of metal instead of a stiff material or whalebone. However, there was a ration on metal during the war, including the metal used in corsets. The decrease in metal usage caused a decline in the number of corsets being produced, pushing the bra to the forefront of the fashion industry.

By the time WWI ended, the Roaring '20s were in full swing. Women's fashion was changing again. The dresses were shorter and more comfortable. Women felt they had gained a little independence from society's oppressive fashion expectations.

Fashion now focused on fewer curves and a flatter chest. The corset was out, and bras that bound the breast were in. (History always repeats itself; remember the women from ancient Greece?) This meant bras needed a snug fit around the bust to smash one's breasts and make them appear smaller. The bras of the 1920s are more commonly called bandeau or tube bras. These bras were made of a tighter material that flattened the breasts and made in a one-size-fits-all pattern (Crandall, 2018).

However, a one-size-fits-all approach does not work for all women. In 1922, New York dress-shop owners Enid Bisset and Ida Rosenthal created a line of bras sewn into dresses. Customers loved these bras and started asking for them to be separated from the dresses so they could be worn with other outfits. This led to the bras being given as a "gift with purchase." This sales technique proved so successful that Ida and Enid — along with Ida's husband, William — started a separate bra company, Maidenform, which remains in existence today.

Enid and Ida chose the name "Maidenform" as an intentional move to maintain a distance from the current fashion trend of the flat-chested flapper look. This line of bras honored a woman's natural body. They came in different shapes and sizes and had individual cups for each breast, which offered more comfort than the tube bras (Maidenform, Inc. History, n.d.). Although the fashion trend of the '20s still favored the small-chested look, with Maidenform, women could purchase bras that had a better fit and greater comfort.

Bras constantly were evolving to reflect the rapid changes in fashion trends and society's expectations of the feminine body. By the '30s, the flapper trend had run its course, and bras were consistently made with individual cups. The new craze was a repeat from history and returned to highlighting a curvier body. Girdles (a lightweight garment that smooths and slims the body) were worn along with bras to emphasize the body's curves (the outline of one's body) and the fullness of the breasts. The bra industry developed a standardized numbered measurement to help women determine the size of bra they needed. A number represented the size of the band (that fits around your chest and clasps), while a letter was assigned to the cup (which held the breast). (Remember my 32A? The diameter of my chest was 32 inches for the band, and A was my cup size.)

During the '30s, Helene Pons patented one of the most common parts of the modern-day bra: the underwire. Underwire is a thin piece of u-shaped metal or plastic inserted into the seam of the bra that cups the breast. Pons' invention offered support, lift and separation of the breasts. However, the look did not take off until after World War II — both when metal was more available and, coincidentally, after the 1943 movie "The Outlaw" starring Jane Russell. The director for this movie wanted Russell's striking silhouette emphasized. Therefore, a bra with underwire was designed for her to wear during the film to give the desired effect. However, Russell didn't like the design and used her own bras, giving them more padding (The Outlaw, 2015). These are the bras she wore in the movie (insert female smirk here).

The 1940s produced one of the weirdest bras ever, the infamous bullet bra. This bra was stiff and pointy, thus its name (and I have to say, this trend makes me crinkle my nose and roll my eyes). Ads for the bra claimed the new shape offered protection for women working in the factories during World War II (Crandall, 2018). Thankfully, the 1960s softened things and bras reflected a more natural bustline. During this time, women started questioning the bra's purpose — many of them daring to wonder whether bras were something they actually needed to wear. Women always have been their own best advocates.

The Women's Liberation Movement has been present throughout history. Women fought for the right to vote, work and manage their own money. However, during the late '60s (and throughout the '80s), the empowerment movement burst through mainstream America in full force. Women demanded equal pay, childcare and workplace advancements. In addition, many women would protest inequality by participating in bra burnings. This act was a symbolic move to represent the freeing of women from societal and cultural oppression.

In the '70s, there was a rise in personal fitness. However, many women avoided exercise because of the lack of support for the breast. If you do not have the needed support, the up-and-down motion caused by running or heavy cardio exercise can cause breast discomfort. By the end of the decade, runner Lisa Lindahl and her childhood friend, costume designer Polly Smith, along with Smith's colleague Hinda Miller, designed the first-ever bra made for women to wear while running. They called it a Jockbra, later called Jogbra™. It was made from two jockstraps (yes, jockstraps — an undergarment worn by athletes that supports the male genitals) sewn together. It gave Lisa the support she needed while running, and the ladies started a business selling these bras.

At first, sports stores were hesitant to sell the new bra. They did not understand why women needed a bra for running. However, women proved otherwise. They loved the Jogbra™, and, in their first year of business, these young female entrepreneurs sold around 25,000. However, there was one small problem: The Jogbra™ didn't fit or offer enough support for women with larger breasts.

Enter Renelle Braaten, a sports enthusiast who invented the Enell™ bra. This bra was made for larger women. It differed from the Jogbra™ because it was not made of elastic. Instead, a firmer material was used with full coverage in the back. The coverage offered women more support and kept their breasts from moving while running or jumping. The Enell™ bra hit the market in 1992. In 2004, Oprah Winfrey endorsed it, thus cementing its place in the history books (Bastone, 2017).

There now are more than 30 different bra designs for women to wear.
From band bras to sports bras, t-shirt bras to bralettes, bras represent many
things to women: freedom, oppression, beauty, discomfort, support, even
annoyance. Yet, despite freeing women from the misery of the corset, they
still can be viewed as restrictive.

But I wonder, does it have to be good or bad? Can bras be seen as something
in between? I mean, if girls and women are the ones who wear bras, then
shouldn't the individual be able to decide what the bra means to her —
and why she may or may not choose to wear it?

## THE PUSHUP BRA
The Truth Under the Padding: Changing the Conversation About Bras

The creation of the bra came from the belief that women needed to shape,
cover, bind or enhance their breasts. We don't need to do any of those things
if we don't want to. It really is that simple. There is no real reason for a woman
to wear a bra unless she wants to. Yes, some women have bigger busts and want
or need breast support. Yes, when our breasts first grow, they are tender, and
we may wish for some cover and support. However, one girl or woman wanting
a bra does not mean that all girls and women must wear them.

Here is the truth of the matter: Bras are innocent. It's people who restrict
one another. We push our opinions onto each other and don't stop to think
that our opinions often are judgments. No one may judge a woman for not
wearing a bra. In its natural state, a feminine body is braless. If this shocks us,
we desperately need to change the conversation. Is it fair to judge someone for
not wearing an item of clothing that makes her feel uncomfortable or
that is unnecessary?

*Sweet Girls,*

*You were made to be you. You were made to be comfortable in your own skin and love your body. Loving your body only happens when you are comfortable in it. So, first, you must believe that you and your body are enough. You are enough.*

*You are enough.*

*You.*
*Are.*
*Enough.*

*Furthermore, you always will be enough. Do not let anyone decide for you how and when you need to support, shape, bind or enhance your breasts. This is up to you. Everyone else's opinions must fall to the wayside.*

*Sometimes we have to follow dress codes that don't make space for personal choice. This makes deciding to wear a bra different from removing body hair or wearing makeup. Therefore, changing the conversation about bras is essential. When everyone understands bras are an option and not an expectation, dress codes will offer more choices.*

## T-Shirt Bras or Bralettes
What to Wear or ... Not Wear

Parents,

Wearing a bra is a complicated issue. Our society is hard-wired to believe feminine breasts should be covered, yet we do not expect men with large breasts to cover theirs. Bras are a part of our dress-code policies at school or at work, and we don't always have the freedom to choose. I realize I am asking us to change a conversation that many of us are uncomfortable changing. So, let's focus on changing the conversation about what our girls wear outside of work, school or church. If our daughters are uncomfortable in bras, can we be "okay" with them going braless when they are not in a formal setting?

As a parent, I want my daughter to dress appropriately for every situation she encounters. When I object to something she is wearing or not wearing, I have to remember to pause and invite myself to figure out why I feel tension around her choices. Is it truly because it is not appropriate attire for the occasion, age or body? Or is it because I have an unfair expectation of the feminine body that was taught to me by our fashion culture? My daughter never really wanted a bra. She simply agreed because that was the only option I gave her. In fact, she was the one who pointed out to me that there were boys with breasts bigger than hers who didn't have to wear a bra. She had a point. But I still wanted her in one because I thought that was the "proper" thing to do. I was wrong, and I owed her an apology. I made an unfair choice because I was afraid of what other girls and women would think of her (and, therefore, me). I used fear as a decision-maker. I let fear of judgment influence my mothering, and that was wrong.

I received my fashion lessons from *Tiger Beat* and *Seventeen* magazines. On TV, I carefully watched Kelly and Brenda from "Beverly Hills, 90210." Our society had different fashion expectations in the '80s and '90s. It is unfair of me to expect my daughter to ignore today's fads in favor of my old-school cultural expectations. I remember arguing with my mother about fashion. There were issues that my mother relented on and things she did not. For example, she insisted I show up to church in a dress, my bright-blue heeled "Sunday Shoes," and hateful bunched-around-the-waist-pantyhose. This was my official church outfit until the seventh grade. However, during my senior year of high school, she let me walk out of the house in a pair of short white shorts and a shirt that barely covered my midriff.

Since I didn't discover beautiful, fun bras until my 16th year, going without a bra never entered my mind until I was an adult. Yet, it's none of my business if my daughter wants to go without. Despite American culture teaching me that wearing a bra was a sign of proper manners, I now realize that one can be proper, professional and bra-less. I remain an expert in my field without wearing a bra. Bras don't make me more intelligent or more efficient at work. Also, if a person wanted to criticize me because the outline of my breast can be seen through my shirt, then that is on him or her. You can see an outline of men's breasts too. Also, what does it mean to be proper? Could we, perhaps, entertain the notion that there are many ways to be proper?

## NATURAL-FITTING BRAS
Things to Ponder While Deciding if Bras Are Right for You

Reasons for wearing a bra:
• Just because.
• You are curious.
• When your breasts are sore and/or need support.
• When you exercise.

When it is time to consider if a bra is right for you:
• When there is breast growth.
• Before puberty.
• After puberty.
• During puberty.
• Whenever you want. You can go your whole life wearing a bra and, at age 63, stop. You can spend your teen years not wearing a bra and, at 23, you may decide to wear one. Any time is the right time to wear (or not wear) a bra.

Here are some things to consider when deciding if a bra is right for you:
• Do you know the correct size bra to purchase?
• Do you know how to measure yourself for a bra?
  (see chart at the end of the book)
• What type of support do you want from a bra?
• Are you familiar with the different types of bras?
• Are you comfortable talking about this subject with your parents?

Parents,

This conversation can be a befuddling one. Go with your gut, love and grace. If you make a wrong move, apologize and tell her this is new territory for you. She will understand. When helping your daughter think through the "to wear or not to wear" process, ask yourself these questions:

• How do you (mom/dad) feel about bras?

• Do you (mom/dad) feel they are a necessary part of a woman's outfit?

• How would you feel if your daughter said she did not want to wear a bra?

1. Why?

2. Are your answers based on fact or opinion?

3. If they are based on opinion, are you prepared to support your daughter if her views differ from your own?

• Moms: Why do/don't you wear a bra?

• Dads: Do you expect women to wear bras? Why or why not?


Normally, this is where I would interject, "If you are like me and have a son … " but this conversation gets tricky. You don't want to embarrass anyone; yet, if your son and husband go shirtless, shouldn't we address the fact that girls and women have to wear shirts? When my son got his puberty talk, we addressed this. We talked about how his pectoral muscles will grow and how we all have breasts, but women typically grow larger breasts so they can feed babies. We also talked about how women's breasts are sexualized and men's aren't — as well as how women are expected to cover and shape their breasts and men aren't, and how this isn't the case in many European countries. So, again, go with your gut, be honest, and just be real. Help him realize bras are cultural. They are options, not expectations.


## The Land of Many Bras
Getting Acquainted With a Bra


How to measure your bra size:
You will need to measure yourself without clothing or bra.

Use a soft measuring tape for your band size and wrap it just under your breasts where the breast and torso meet. The measuring tape should lay flat against your skin. Do not pull it tight around you. Where the measuring tape comes together, note the number; that is your band size. If you get an odd number, move up to the following even number.

To get your cup size, you will need to wrap the measuring tape around the fullest part of your bust. Note the number; that is your bust measurement. Next, subtract the band size from the bust measurement. The difference between the two measurements will give you your cup size on the chart below.

For example, if your band size is 36 and your bust measurement is 38, you are a 36B.

Difference  Cup Size

| | | | | | |
|---|---|---|---|---|---|
| 1" | A | 3" | C | 5" | DD |
| 2" | B | 4" | D | 6" | DDD |

A Little Lace

10 Fun & Slightly Crazy Facts About Bras

- During WWI, enough metal was collected from corsets to make 2 battleships.
- Neil Armstrong's space suit was created by seamstresses from Playtex, a bra manufacturer.
- Televised bra commercials could not show real women wearing bras until 1987.
- A study from 2013 found that the average bra size is 34DD.
- Mark Twain, the storyteller and poet, patented the modern-day bra clasp.
- During the 1940s, many women made their own bras.
- A good bra can last from six to nine months.
- The oldest known bra is approximately 600 years old.

• The average woman has anywhere from 8-16 bras but only wears about
  4 of them.

• The most expensive bra is priced at $12.5 million.

## LESS BINDING & MORE LOVE
Women Who Are Taking Back the Business of Bras

### Ade Hassan, Nubian Skin
Ade Hassan is helping the world understand that the word "nude" applies
to all races.

If you wear a bra, there will be times when you need one that matches your
skin tone, as in a nude bra. However, for decades, there only were a handful
of options available for nude bras, and most of those choices were for lighter
skin tones. However, Ade Hassan is broadening our definition of "nude."
She developed a line of bras, lingerie and hosiery that matches darker skin
tones. Her company, Nubian Skin, has a global reach. Her work is making
the world of bras more inclusive for Black and Brown women.

### Heidi Zak, ThirdLove
Heidi Zak is bringing a sigh of relief to the world of bras.

ThirdLove brings love, ease and confidence to the woman in the bra.
Founder Heidi Zak is committed to listening to the needs and wants
of women who wear bras. Her company promotes comfort with a side
of beauty. It is an industry built on supporting women and their bodies.
ThirdLove invests in other women-owned businesses and partners with
organizations that give feminine-hygiene products to girls and women
in need. This business understands that a bra should be comfortable
and supportive instead of a binding and restrictive expectation.

# THE NUMBERS
## — ASSIGNED TO —
# OUR BODIES

CLOTHING & FASHION

FASHION:

The current custom of dress, manner, socializing, etiquette.

CLOTHING:

Garments and/or apparel; a covering.

WHAT I'VE LEARNED:

One does not need to wear the most fashionable clothing to be beautiful.

Chapter 5

## NOT A FASHIONISTA

An Honest Confession of Fashion Fiascos and See-Through Pants

My father was in the Air Force and I spent a big part of my childhood living
in England. From the ages of 8-12, I lived just off an Air Force base in a small
English village. Everything was small, cozy and predictable. I went to school
with other kids whose fathers were in the military. We bought food from the
commissary, went to the same restaurants, the same movie theater and all
of us bought clothes at the base exchange.

Except for my 10th birthday, I got to go to a department store to buy a black
winter coat and a quilted, blue-flowered polyester housecoat. This was the same
housecoat I wore in my fifth-grade school play. I was the Queen of Sweden ...
in a blue-flowered polyester housecoat. Also, my mother was notorious for
making my sister and me dress alike. There was a time she made the three of us
matching dresses. Nothing says "I am a cool 12-year-old" like wearing the same
clothes as your 33-year-old mom and 9-year-old sister. However, she made
me two killer prom dresses!

When we moved back to the States the summer before seventh grade, I walked
off a plane from England in mother/daughter matching dresses — and entered
a world I didn't understand. Life moved so fast in Texas. Everything was loud,
busy and bright. My quiet English life was gone. Everybody dressed differently;
however, in contrast, it seemed you could only be friends with people who
dressed like you. My clothing choices were supposed to fit into one of these

categories: Cowboys, Preps, Punks or Nerds. But, in reality, my clothing didn't look like anything worn by the kids around me.

I showed up for the first day of middle school in a black and white outfit. The pants were white and see-through. Did I mention I hadn't seen the sun in four years? I was pale and wearing white see-through pants with white underwear that you could see (fashion note: unless you want your undies to be seen, wear nude undergarments with white clothing). I had on a black and white blouse with black and white saddle shoes with white socks. It was such an odd choice for the first day of school. If you've read the makeup chapter, you also know I had on clown makeup. My cheeks were a waxy red, and my eyebrows were the same tan color as my lips. Yikes!

Everyone else was in jeans and loafers and girls had elasticized fabric circles in their hair called "scrunchies." But the most confusing thing of all was on the back of the girls' jeans. I kept seeing a small upside-down triangle that said "Guess" on it. I was puzzled at what I was supposed to "guess." (It took me a month before I realized that Guess was the name of a clothing company.) On top of all that, while everyone else had a Texas twang, I spoke slowly and very precisely, without any twang at all. I am sure I looked like a clown-faced ghost. More than once that day, I was told I sounded funny. One kid asked if I was even speaking English.

It was a miserable first day of school.

I spent my teen years chasing down the latest fashions and wearing clothes that didn't quite fit. In college, I wanted to wear clothing with the smallest number on the tag. It is no fun to sit in a three-hour class wearing too-tight jeans. I was in my late 30s when I finally realized that the size of my jeans did not define my worth. This is a hard place to get to, which is why I am including this chapter in Her Story. The story of fashion, clothing and sizes is frustrating. We get too caught up in it all, and it ruins the day. How many of you changed clothes over three times this morning because nothing looked right? Yeah, I know that feeling.

From all of this, I have learned that fashion is all about self-expression. If you dress in a style that you like, then who cares about wearing the latest fashion fad? Clothing and fashion choices should be fluid; you should be able to dress in a manner that reflects your comfort and preferences. In one week I will wear everything from workout clothes to a skirt with heels. It truly depends on what I want to wear and where I go that day. My preferred style of dress? Jeans and a t-shirt. But I love comfortable and quirky shoes. To me, the shoes complete the outfit. I won't sacrifice comfort for fashion, but, girl, I love a fun shoe. When you are confident, it shows through whatever clothes you are wearing. I have learned that I decide for myself what is fashionable, and those ridiculous numbers on jeans are just that — ridiculous.

## Patterns & Fabric
### Fashion With a Side of Feelings

What comes to mind when you hear "fashion" and "clothing?" Do you get excited? Do you love to shop and put together outfits for fun? Do you enjoy accessorizing your outfits? Or do you just feel dread? Do you experience anxiety at not knowing what clothing looks best on you, and do you have trouble deciding what to wear when you go to school or out with friends? Do you feel overwhelmed by the idea of accessorizing? Or are you confused about why clothes don't always come in your size? Do you feel excluded by the fashion industry?

We need to do some severe unpacking (pun intended) around clothing and fashion. These topics can go together like spaghetti and meatballs or completely repel each other, like toothpaste and orange juice. Nevertheless, they are beloved and befuddling parts of beauty culture. It's odd how, on any given day, a pair of jeans can make you feel trendy and empowered or insecure and mad. How much do we let clothing affect our confidence? We need to understand how clothing and fashion affect beauty culture to answer this question. After all, the global fashion industry was worth $2.5 trillion in 2020. The average woman will spend about $100,000 on clothing in her lifetime. If we are going to spend our time, energy and money on clothing purchases, then we had better make some wise choices. It's worth a deep dive.

Sometimes clothing can feel restrictive and fashion overwhelming. What happens when the trendiest fad isn't something you like? Do you feel pressured to wear it? If you don't wear it, does somebody question you about it? How do you answer? Are you honest, or do you feel you have to cover up the truth? What happens when the trendy jeans you long for don't come in the size you are most comfortable wearing?

The fashion industry relies on small bodies to sell clothing for reasons discussed later in this chapter. Fashion magazines hire thin models and edit their pictures to make them even smaller. Then, via airbrushing, they slice off bits of pixelated thigh and tummy to shape and mold the body into their image of perfection — thus brainwashing the rest of our culture into accepting their idea of beauty. Is this the correct and ethical way to sell clothing? Is there a way to make the fashion industry more inclusive?

If the clothing industry makes you feel like:
• You are the wrong weight
• You have the wrong body size
• You don't belong in certain stores
• You never will be able to wear trendy jeans
then we need to change the conversation about clothing and the feminine body. All girls deserve to feel represented in the fashion industry.

To start this conversation, we must travel back through time to understand the origins and history of clothing. We will learn how clothing became a fashion statement and how the sizing system was developed. We also will examine how fashion got tangled up with good manners and proper character. There is a lot of information on clothing. I will keep things light until we hit fashion in the United States and then dive deeper.

Are you ready? Let's begin.

## A Basic Stitch Using Thread & Needle
From Body Coverings to Clothing

Throughout history, people have used clothing as protection, gender expression, self-expression, rebellion, art and comfort. It tells the story of humans, beliefs, mindsets and lifestyles. The clothing evolution started with body coverings, developed into clothing, and finally fashion. Before clothing was used to cover the body, early humans decorated their bodies in various ways. Anthropologists can trace this practice back at least 30,000 years when they found evidence of beads, shells and plants thoughtfully placed on the bodies in gravesites (Monet, 2020).

At first, anthropologists thought clothing protected bodies from nature's elements: heat, cold, rain and snow. Yet, there is evidence of clothing in societies that didn't necessarily need it for protection, like those who live in milder climates. So, I can't help but wonder — was clothing an extension of early humans decorating their bodies?

Early humans covered themselves with materials made from natural resources, such as animal skins and plant fibers. Findings suggest people made rudimentary sewing needles and weaving looms from animal bones to stitch materials together. As time passed and trade routes became established, people had access to more resources to make their coverings. They could now choose durable and comfortable materials that were pleasing to the eye.

This is when body covering became clothing, but not yet fashion (Monet, 2020) (Who invented clothes? A Paleolithic archaeologist answers, 2013).

Functionality remained a determining factor in material choices. Clothing had to allow people to move around quickly as they did their hunting, gathering and farming. It also needed to protect people from the weather. For instance, people who lived in warm climates wore loose clothing made of linen because it doesn't hold heat. In contrast, people in colder climates wore clothing close to the body made of wool or animal skin to keep body heat in.

## MUSLIN & LINEN
### Clothing & Fashion in Ancient Civilizations

Let's jump into the clothing and fashion timeline here. The year is 3150 BCE. The most powerful civilizations are Egypt, Greece and Rome. They all had very similar clothing and were the first civilizations to dress for function and decor. Most clothing was loose-fitting, made from linen or wool, and required some type of sash to fasten or drape the material in elaborate ways — both for style and to indicate one's station in life.

These cultures introduce us to the idea of fashion. Fashion originated when people dressed according to their social classes. The wealthy wore clothing made from the most expensive fabric, which meant it was of higher-quality material and usually more colorful. Not everyone could afford this material or could dress like the noble class. But that didn't stop people from wanting to look like the cool kids. Sound familiar?

In Egypt, men of wealth wore cloth wrapped around their hips. Women wore a close-fitting tube-like dress called a kalasiris. Clothing was made with lightweight fabric for the warm climate. The wealthy could afford to buy dyed fabric for their clothing. The most popular colors were red, yellow, blue and green. Women decorated their dresses with elaborate collars and belts made of colorful materials and jewels (DK Publishing, 2012).

Working-class Egyptians couldn't afford fine clothing. While clothing basics were the same, the material was rough and plain. Their styles had a looser fit without elaborate accessories or belts. Interestingly enough, it doesn't appear that either class cared about footwear. However, when needed, sandals were the preferred choice (Egyptian Footwear, n.d.).

Greek men and women had the same basic garment as the foundation of their clothing. However, women wore their tunics looser than their Egyptian sisters. The Greek people draped and accessorized their togas and tunics for dramatic fashion effects. The fabric would change depending on the weather: heavier for colder temperatures and lighter material for warmer days. Sandals were the preferred choice when shoes were worn.

Roman men and women preferred togas with sashes or decorated ties. Their togas likely were made of spun wool, more so for men than women. Men wore either tunics or togas — the toga was the longer, more formal of the two choices. Like their Egyptian sisters, Roman women wore their tunics with a closer fit, highlighting their bodies. The material was lighter and often more colorful. It was important for a Roman woman to dress in a manner that showcased her family's fortune.

Married women wore stolas over their togas. A stola was a dress that was worn over the toga and flowed to the floor. Many women received one as a wedding gift. The last bit of clothing a Roman woman wore was a palla, or shawl worn over the shoulders. Wealthy women had beautifully made pallas, while women in the working classes had plain ones. So, again, we see the difference in dress between the classes that was the basis of fashion trends (Women's Clothes in Ancient Rome, 2018).

In Asia, regulations and formalities around clothing kept the social classes and professions separated. The loose-fitting tunic was the basis for most outfits in China. The working class wore light-colored clothing made of hemp or plant fibers, but the wealthy wore delicate, dark-colored fabrics such as silk. Over their tunics they layered expensive fabrics, draping them into fashionable folds with ties (Ancient Chinese Clothing, n.d.). The famous Japanese kimono appeared first in history in 794 C.E. Adapted through the years, it is a mainstay of Japanese fashion.

Unlike other civilizations we read about, people regularly wore shoes in China. While there is a plethora of information about them, I will focus on a fascinating — albeit stomach-twisting — fact about shoes and foot binding. During this time, Chinese people considered tiny feet an attractive quality in women, much like a small waist was desirable in European cultures. When a girl was born, her toes were bound under her feet to make them smaller. Eventually, toes grew under the foot, forever hobbling the girl. Her shoes reflected the minuscule feet they encased. Footwear was indeed small, made with elaborate stitching and intricate patterns, possessing an almost doll-like quality. Unfortunately, shoes for girls and women were more for show than for use (Foreman, 2015).

## Wool Tunics

### A Brief History of Clothing Trends in Europe

Let's take a big jump in time to the Middle Ages in Europe, roughly 476 C.E.-1453 C.E. People still are wearing tunics. Much like today's fashion, clothing during the Middle Ages went through different trends and phases. It started with both men and women in various forms of tunics and slowly, over the centuries, clothing developed into very distinct styles for the genders. At this point, the details and history of clothing can start to feel vast and overwhelming. To simplify things, we will concentrate on women's clothing for the rest of the chapter.

English life was hard in the Middle Ages. There were sicknesses, heavy taxes, strict laws, and people had to work exhaustively to make a living. It didn't help that the climate was cold and wet. Clothing had to be heavy and durable to withstand the weather and harsh lifestyles. Female family members or servants made most dresses in the home. Clothes still separated social classes. However, by this point in history, dyes were commonplace and easy to create using plants, making colorful clothing possible for everyone.

As I stated earlier, at the beginning of the Middle Ages, women wore loose-fitting, long-sleeved tunics gathered at the waist with belts. Over time, women wore more formal and fitted gowns over their tunics. Many tunics now were sleeveless and functioned more like undergarments instead of outerwear. As time went on, women added yet another more formal layer of clothing over their dresses. This was a fitted outer dress called a surcoat (or surcote). Surcoats were made with heavier material and often sported broad, long sleeves that sometimes touched the ground.

Toward the end of the 14th century, women wore very full gowns made with a generous amount of fabric — and these were called houppelandes. Women paired this with an underdress that peeked out between the belted folds of the houppelande. Due to the amount of material used for this type of dress, it was the most expensive gown of the Middle Ages.

Women of noble class or royalty accessorized their clothes with jewels, intricate stitching or gold embroidery. Their clothing was bright and made of expensive fabrics like silk or taffeta, lined with fur or camel hair to help keep them warm. A tailor typically made their clothing to ensure a good fit (Gilbert, n.d.).

In the working or peasant classes, women usually farmed, worked in their husbands' trades, or gained employment as servants in wealthy households.

They made their own garments at home using wool or linen. Because of being hand-sewn, clothing was durable enough to withstand the hardships of peasant life.

The lower classes attempted to follow the fashion trends of the wealthy. However, they couldn't afford expensive fabrics, dyes or embroidery. In truth, lower-class women had little need for costly gowns because of their complex lives. Working-class women did not own as much clothing as their wealthy counterparts, which meant they had to be extra-careful in making their dresses because clothing had to last a long time (Gilbert, n.d.).

The sumptuary laws were another barrier that the working class had to navigate when choosing to clothe themselves. The dates of these laws stretched from Roman times throughout the 1700s. Their purpose was to instill strong moral and ethical habits in people by prohibiting them from excessive spending and indulgent tastes. In addition, these laws told people what they could and could not wear. So, even if members of the peasantry could afford expensive materials to make a dress, they couldn't purchase or wear it (Sumptuary Laws of the Middle Ages, 2017).

Finally, the shoes. Shoes were essential during this time; the climate often was cold, there was a lot of mud, and being barefoot was a sign of poverty. Typically, shoes were made of leather, with little difference between men's and women's shoes. There were ankle boots, full-size boots, sandals, and an early form of slippers (Medieval Shoes, 2020). (It wasn't until the 13th century that shoes were made specifically for right and left feet.) High heels appeared in Europe after the Middle Ages, more specifically in the early 17th century. Introduced by Persian emissaries, wealthy men wore them to show off their status (Kremer, 2013). Of course, they looked nothing like they do today. Initially, high heels were for men and not women. Men wore them when riding horses, as the heel helped the rider keep a tight hold on his horse by keeping the foot from slipping out of the stirrup. The heel also gave a man extra height (Wynne, 2017).

The first woman to wear high heels was our corset-loving friend, Catherine de Medici, in the 16th century — she wanted to appear taller at her wedding (Wynne, 2017). However, once high heels became a fashion statement, people wore them as accessories rather than necessities. As a result, the style often was over-the-top. Usually, the person wearing the shoe needed help walking because it was so impractical — which isn't that different from some of the high heels we have today! However, soon we will see how shoes will become a mainstay of the fashion world.

The Renaissance Era, which is believed to have begun in Italy after the Middle Ages and spread throughout the rest of Europe until the beginning of the 17th century, celebrated a time of rebirth and renewal. People were casting off the old, heavy thoughts and beliefs of the Middle Ages, and clothing was evolving. Royalty still set fashion standards and, no matter one's class or belief system, the dresses remained big and bulky. They covered women's arms, at least to their elbows, and the entire length of their legs. Corsets became standard for women, and shoes took on a fashion life of their own. It was not uncommon for both men and women to wear corsets and high heels until the latter part of the 1800s.

During the 1700s, clothing became very fashionable. The popular style was baroque or rococo; it was a flamboyant trend. Clothing colors favored pastel shades with whimsical flair. The necklines of dresses became very relaxed and revealing. A curious trend during this time was the use of panniers. Women wore side hoops, or "false hips," that extended the look of their actual hips (McNamara, 2018). Wearing these panniers made the front and back of their bodies appear flat. The trend was extreme. Many women had trouble fitting through doors, sitting in chairs and walking downstairs. They also had to put up with men grumbling about the amount of space their dresses took up in a room (Major Fashion Trends and Styles of the 1700s, n.d.). (Hey, maybe the guys had a point.) Along with panniers, the length of the skirt became shorter — revealing a lady's stockings and shoes. This led to shoes becoming more of a fashion statement and receiving their own flamboyant designs and colors. This trend ended during the French Revolution, and simpler styles returned.

## HOOP SKIRTS, BARE ARMS & NUMBERS
America Steps Into the World of Fashion

From Europe to the U.S.

When Europeans first came to the new land, fashion had to take a backseat as people figured out how to live a new life. Clothing was simple. The styles reflected one's belief system or the sumptuary laws. The newcomers also had a limited supply of clothing and material with which to work. It took a while to adjust to their new ways of life in the American colonies. But, slowly, people became familiar and comfortable with their new home — and, with that, the wealthier families started setting new fashion standards. Often, the trends in America came from Europe. A woman traveling abroad would see something she liked, buy it, and take it back home — where others would see it and copy it. If something was in fashion, you wanted to conform to the trend to show you had fashion sense. Fitting in with society was a must for women who wanted to marry.

People cared about what women wore because clothing reflected their beauty and morality. A woman's job was to raise a family. People wanted mothers to have a solid ethical and moral character. A woman needed to attract and marry a husband by following the expectations society had laid out for her, which included ways of dressing.

Dresses were carefully hand-sewn using needle and thread. This process was tiresome, as it took a great deal of time and energy to sew just one dress. However, in 1846, Elias Howe invented the first sewing machine, which featured the stitch-locking method still used in machines today. But, in 1851, Isaac Singer topped Howe's invention by patenting a machine that added a foot pedal and refined the needle and stitching. As a result, Singer mass-produced sewing machines, paying royalty fees to Howe. Thanks to the ingenuity of Howe and

Singer, tailors and seamstresses could build up their businesses and create more clothing. Singer sewing machines remain in production today (Bellis, 2019).

By the mid-1800s, differing lifestyles and political views between the North and South kept the country divided. Women's fashion choices reflected the difference. Wealthy women from the South wore a style of dress that originated in Victorian England. The traditional dress was the classic hoop skirt, tight corset, stockings, bloomers, petticoats and buttoned bodices. The hoop skirt gave women a bell shape; thus, they were called Southern belles. The girth of the dresses meant that staircases and doorways needed to be wide so a woman could fit through them. Homes of that time were built to allow for the fullness of a woman's gown.

Seamstresses or enslaved women made clothing in the home. This meant the dresses fit a lady's body precisely. When new fashion trends rose, old dresses were redesigned into new fads instead of shopping for a different dress. Material from old gowns was recycled to make clothes for the children in the family.

Women who farmed or worked in their husbands' businesses wore a fashion similar to this, but not nearly as fancy. Their dresses had to allow for the high level of work required for their ways of life. Hoop skirts were not an option for them. Instead, they wore cotton dresses, often with interchangeable sleeves. Women could interchange their sleeves to accessorize their dresses. There still were many layers under the dress — and most women wore corsets.

Enslaved women had to wear whatever clothing the plantation owners gave them. Typical attire would be simple, long-sleeved cotton dresses and aprons. On average, enslaved people received clothing once a year and often owned fewer than three outfits. As a result, they had to take care of their clothing to make it last as long as possible (Monet, 2020).

Women in northern cities wanted to set themselves apart from those in the South. They did this in subtle ways. Clothing in the North did not have the colorful flair of the South. Women had to walk down the crowded city streets, and their houses were smaller, so their skirts were not as full. In fact, public transportation in New York charged more for women in hoop skirts because they took up more space (Green, 2012). There was racism in the North, but slavery did not exist. Women of color dressed in styles similar to those of White women.

Women also had to be careful about getting the hems of their dresses dirty as they walked along the unpaved streets. City streets were muddy and full of horse manure, as horse-drawn carriages were the primary mode of transportation. This led to northern hemlines being shorter than southern hemlines.

There are three things I find very intriguing about this period. The first is the strict etiquette centered on different clothing for different daily activities. For example, if you needed to go into town for an errand, you changed clothes. You didn't go to the market wearing a regular day dress. Instead, you had dresses specifically for traveling into town. Also, when it was time for dinner, families would change out of their day clothes into more formal attire for dinner.

The second was the lack of independence women had when dressing. Their many layers of clothing, hoop skirts, tight corsets and intricate buttons meant they needed help — every time they dressed and undressed. It also required time and patience to put on, pin and tie each layer of clothing. Women and girls couldn't run upstairs to quickly change for dinner. Instead, they had to plan a time to change their dresses every day. (I wonder: How much time did they spend dressing and undressing? Yikes!)

As for the third, many terms and mindsets that focus on modesty, purity and innocence of young ladies came from this era. Etiquette books advised women that corsets were not to be "loose" on a woman. Her body must be "properly restrained" in her clothing and hold her "upright" (Green, 2012). Unfortunately, these terms became less about the clothing and more about the girl or woman. Loose implied a lady who wanted to attract men, but a restrained and upright young lady was of good character; she could control her thoughts and urges. People felt they could tell a young girl's personality by the way she dressed. This is a mindset that still restrains girls and women today.

Let me add an extra thought: Women's clothing was pocket-free, forcing a lady to rely on a bag (the origin of purses) or a man who had pockets in his clothing to hold her things. This made her dependent on others while she was out. With apparel, women had very little independence.

Let's jump back across the pond to Europe for a bit. In the mid- to late-1800s, an elite line of fashion houses started in Paris. These houses specialized in tailor-made clothing for women of wealth. They were called haute couture (high-fashion design) and were led by fashion designers. The houses were required to employ 20 seamstresses and debut 35 new items of clothing each season (The History of Haute Couture, 2017). Initially, fashion designers used mannequins to show off their new clothing lines during a debut. Decades later (we are stepping out of our timeline and following a tangent here), live mannequins (or models) were incorporated into the debuts — marking the beginning of the modeling profession.

Designers wanted the live models to wear clothing like a mannequin to show the audience what the clothes looked like in action. They wanted people to notice how the fabric moved and cascaded down the body. However, designers also wanted the audience to picture themselves in the dresses. This, Sweet Girls, is why fashion designers want small bodies. Small bodies can be invisible as the clothing walks down the runway: Models are living clothes hangers. Haute couture influenced fashion worldwide, thus setting standards for the feminine body today. Later in this chapter, we will talk about how these standards have affected the beauty culture but, for now, let's get back to the late 1800s in the United States.

The Civil War forced a change in fashion and clothing. With so many men off fighting the war, women had to take on many responsibilities at home. They soon realized hoop skirts hindered their ability to get work done.

So, hoop skirts were out — but the layers of petticoats, bloomers and corsets stayed. Dresses still were elegant, but now they were narrow. This fashion carried women through to the early 1900s, then everything changed, and the fashion world turned upside down.

As mentioned in almost every chapter, in 1908, French clothing designer Paul Poiret introduced the world to a fashion craze it never had seen before. He reconstructed the Victorian-inspired dresses of the day, making them light and loose. In doing so, he freed the arms, legs, waists and busts of women. Moreover, he gave women a dose of daring with a side of independence.

Victorian dresses were tailored to create an hourglass figure for women. They gave the illusion of a big bust, small waist and wide hips, whereas Poiret's new dresses took shape out of a woman's body by softening the curves of the dress and removing the waistline. He created clothing that draped and flowed around a woman. A Poiret creation didn't encase her body in layers of restrictive fabric. It was a radical change in the current mindset and purpose of fashion. Until this point, style reflected a woman's moral character. Now women were wearing dresses that didn't accommodate a corset. Instead, they revealed their arms and ankles. It was a fashion upheaval that occurred right on the cusp of the First World War.

Let's take a break from the history of clothing and talk about what's bubbling underneath the world of fashion: department stores and magazines. These two entities are crucial because they are part of why we have numbers assigned to our bodies.

As stated before, dresses were made in the home by someone familiar to the girl or woman. Mercantile stores would sell material and embellishments to make dresses. Perhaps some stores would sell dresses but, typically, clothing was made by hand for a specific girl's or woman's body (Brumberg, 1998).

However, with the invention of the sewing machine, garment businesses were on the rise. Chicago was the first city to see a boom in this industry. In 1860, the clothing industry started making men's clothing. About 10 years later, women's clothing started being mass-produced. By the end of the 1800s, Chicago continued to lead the industry in men's clothing, and New York was the epicenter for women's fashion (Bae, n.d.).

The rise of the garment industry meant all those clothes needed a place to be sold. Enter department stores. With the increase in the garment industry, department stores were the perfect place to sell clothing. But, how would people find clothing that fit their bodies in a department store? This led the garment industry to attempt a universal sizing system using age, meaning a 13-year-old would wear a size 13. Unfortunately, this didn't always work out well. No two 13-year-olds are exactly alike, and clothing still needed to be taken to a tailor for alterations. Also, at what age does one stop making clothing sizes that conform to ages? Underneath this new department-store phenomenon was a rising self-consciousness. Girls were comparing themselves to others.

Clothing made at home had no "size." The person making the dress would take a girl's measurements, but those measurements weren't a "size." They were just the measurements of that particular body. But one did have to be aware of sizes when buying clothing at a store. Instead of the dress fitting the body, the body now has to fit the dress. The garment industry determined the size of the body. Going shopping for dresses made girls and women aware of the sizes of other girls and women. Size consciousness was now a thing. Shopping invited girls to compare themselves to one another.

Furthermore, for women who did not live near a department store, there were magazines with pictures or illustrations of models. Women would look through magazines to find the things they wanted or needed and mail in an order form, and their purchases were sent back to them. The models in the magazines always were beautiful, with sleek waists, slender arms and thin legs. The dresses fit them perfectly. So imagine a young girl's surprise and frustration when she received the dress and it didn't fit her like it fit the model in the magazine.

A wave of self-conscious comparison slowly spread across the United States. For the first time in history, we see a rise in body negativity (Brumberg, 1998). Poiret's current fashion trend accelerated this. As wonderful as it was to have a dress that freed women from the corset, the flip side was that it required bodies to be small and shapeless. It was designed to hang off the shoulders and float around the body. At first, it was clothing that was seen as a fashion statement — but now the body was part of the package. This is the first time in history where there is documentation of young girls actively trying to lose weight. Fashion insisted that they fit their natural, beautiful curves into a curve-less dress ... and no one talked about it.

Let's step back into our timeline. We now are in the trenches of World War I. Fashion was put on hold as Americans figured out how to live in a world at war. Dresses became simpler for several reasons:
1. It felt like bad manners to dress in elegant wear when your country was at war.
2. Women were stepping back into the workforce just as they did during the Civil War to provide for their families while the men fought in Europe.
3. The government placed a ration on many fabrics and materials used for clothing.

Once the war was over, fashion took another giant step forward. Ladies, let's meet The Flapper. We have talked about her in previous chapters, but now we get to formally meet her. She is curiously exquisite and redefined what it meant to be a woman.

The Flapper — a name whose origin has not been pinned down — referred to a woman who lived unconventionally. She was adventurous and unconcerned with society's strict moral etiquette for women. This woman went to jazz clubs, drove cars, wore makeup and made up her own mind. She wore dresses that showed off her legs, shoulders and arms. She may not have worn a bra, and she didn't care if other women judged her for it. Flappers were done with being told what to do and how to act. They were ready to live life by their own rules.

They got a reputation for being irresponsible and having poor character, but that was the point. Women were unfairly judged for doing the same things that men did. Men drove cars and went to jazz clubs, but nobody looked down on them. These women wanted their independence without judgment and were determined to get it.

Companies took notice of this lifestyle and started advertising to these free spirits. Ads for makeup, razors, perfume, hair products, dresses and bras (instead of corsets) increased. Magazines were full of opportunities for women to buy into flapper fashion, and young women embraced it. They finally had a moment of true freedom. By 1920, women had worked to pass the 19th amendment, which gave most women the right to vote. They had entered the workforce and had money to spend on exciting new fashion trends.

As the '20s gave way to the '30s, dresses began embracing curves again. The Great Depression engulfed the whole decade, and clothing remained simple, with straight-lined dresses and few embellishments. However, there was one article of clothing introduced to women during the '30s. In 1934, Levi's pants company introduced the world to Lady Levi's jeans, made exclusively for women. Pants for women weren't really a "thing," and no one had even heard of women wearing jeans. However, with the introduction of blue jeans, the idea of pants for women was not far off!

In 1939, The Agriculture Department launched a year-long study called The Women's Measurements for Garment and Pattern Construction. More than 14,000 women submitted their height, bust, waist and hip measurements. The results were used to help improve pattern production. (Patterns are used to make clothing.) However, the study required women to be White, and any measurements collected from women of color were disregarded (Robinson 2016). So, once again, the bodies of women of color were ignored.

This study will come up in history again. So, hang on to this knowledge as we step into the '40s.

The 1940s brought World War II, a skirt suit for women, dress pants, and Rosie the Riveter. With the United States in another war, women once again were taking charge of things on the home front. They went into the office wearing skirts that stopped at the knees or wide-leg pants with a high waist. In factories, women proudly donned denim as they worked on production lines. Curves were still en vogue. Women in suit jackets with shoulder pads kept businesses running. In contrast, ladies in jeans and bandanas kept America's military stocked in planes, tanks and boats.

Fashion trends of the 1950s were a mix of old fads with a new flair. Women and girls could wear full or pencil skirts. The garment industry produced capris, blouses, sweaters, elegant gowns, day dresses, shorts and high-waisted jeans. Hemlines were short, long, or somewhere in between. Petticoats made skirts float about the body, girdles squeezed torsos, and bras made breasts appear bigger. Department stores were booming with clothing options. These fashion trends continued into the '60s, eventually colliding with the hippie.

Before we step into the '60s and '70s, do you remember those clothing measurements from the study in 1939? In 1953, they were used to create a sizing system. This included reducing the amount of clothing made by the garment industry by using every other number as a size. To further complicate things, the industry decided that women would feel better about themselves if the number on their clothes was smaller than their actual size. As a result, companies adjusted clothing sizes to favor this practice we now call vanity sizing. While it seemed pretty harmless at first, this idea has reinforced the opinion that a smaller body is a better body (Robinson, n.d.). By 1958, the U.S. had a standard sizing chart that has changed very little in the past 63 years — meaning that women of color were left out of the sizing system,

and larger bodies of any color are expected to be content with fewer items
of clothing available for them.

The hippies of the late '60s and '70s rejected the ideas of traditional America.
They didn't believe in war, or that success came from high-paying 9-to-5 jobs.
Instead, they had their own belief system, behaviors and style. "Peace, love
and acceptance" was their motto. Their casual, offbeat clothes directly opposed
department-store swank. Their peaceful beliefs opened doors for mainstream
America to accept a more relaxed fashion attitude.

At the same time, we have the first hip-hugging bell-bottom jeans, short
shorts and miniskirts that put teenage girls into a fashion craze all over the
United States. Jeans paired with a t-shirt now were a lovable combo that had
a spot in every kid's closet.

As we move into the '80s, '90s and beyond, we have our first look at punk,
grunge and everything in between. Girls wore corsets as shirts, paired with
neon micro miniskirts. Oversized jeans and shirts became fads. Sneakers were
both fashion statements and indications of wealth. Flannel shirts over bodysuits
and cowboy boots and belt buckles became attractive. These new trends blurred
the lines of what was and wasn't stylish. We relied on trips to the mall with
friends to help us find our perfect fashion statement.

It is here that we restrain ourselves again. We shop not only for clothes
but also for society's approval. We let others tell us whether we look good in
something. In fact, we scroll through TikTok and Instagram just to see what
others are wearing. We look at celebrities' fashion choices, judge them, envy
them and eventually copy them. But then we think we can evaluate the
fashion choices of others.

Yet again, we have corseted ourselves, and it's time to change the conversation.

# The Underside of a Stitch

The Not-So-Pretty Side to Fashion  — Changing the Conversation

Society, haute couture, and the garment industry tied women's bodies to fashion for too long.

If these entities were being honest, they would have told us:

We used fashion to create an exclusive girls' club. We wanted you to covet this elite space and willingly pay whatever it took to get in. We wanted small bodies in our clothes because we liked how the fabric hung. It helped that people paid attention to the clothes and not the girl in the clothes. Your payment into our elite club was your body and your confidence. As you eased and squeezed into our jeans, we whispered, "Leave your confidence in the fitting room. Let us make you feel good with our clothing." Your ticket to our club was the number we assigned to your body. We didn't care if we left a body out, and we certainly didn't care if we made you feel like your body was wrong, damaged, too big, too tall, too short or too small. We, the fashion industry, feasted on your insecurities, your self-perceived imperfections, and your desire to fit in with other girls. We are sorry.

We are sorry we used fashion to cover, smother and restrain you. We are sorry we made you doubt the size and shape of your body. We are sorry we made you believe that you must cover all of your body to be proper. To be considered a free spirit, you must let your arms and legs be free. To be attractive, you must show your skin. To be beautiful, you must have a small, invisible body. We are sorry we confused and manipulated you with clothing. Clothing is a basic need, and we got carried away. You don't need our help to be beautiful or confident. You are beautiful because you are you.

That's what they should be saying.

*Sweet Girls,*

*You are fashionable. You entered the world with flair, grace and beauty. Fashion is about expressing yourself. Confidence comes from your spirit, not from your clothing. When clothing and fashion came together, somehow they spun our bodies into the mix. Suddenly, the outfit became more important than the body. This is backward thinking. Your body always comes first, and it does not have to meet the fashion standards of others. You are enough. You are enough. You. Are. Enough. Do not let the fashion industry tell you differently.*

When choosing clothes for yourself:
- Never mind the number; it is arbitrary, and chances are it changes depending on the store you visit.
- Wear clothing that feels comfortable and expresses your personality.
- Wear clothing that allows your confidence to shine through.
- Wear clothing that doesn't match, if that's what makes you happy.
- Experiment with clothes and accessories.
- You can have as many styles as you want.
- Just because something is fashionable doesn't mean you have to wear it.
- Learn to ask yourself if you like what you are wearing before asking others. Also, if you like it, why bother to ask others?
- It is okay to get help when putting together an outfit.
- Learn to trust your own judgment.
- If an outfit makes you doubt yourself, it's not for you.

## SHORT DRESSES OR LONG PANTS
How to Navigate the World of Fashion

Parents,

Helping our girls navigate clothing and fashion can be complex. I will admit that some places require us to wear specific clothing items that our girls may find uncomfortable, such as uniforms at school, church clothing, or formal wear for special occasions. However, when we give our girls guidance and freedom to dress as they wish during their off time, it makes those times when dress codes are required easier to manage.

I never will forget when I took my daughter shopping for an Easter dress. She was in the fourth grade, and neither of us was looking forward to the outing. Every time we had to buy her clothes, we ended up fighting. I was pretty thankful that her school had a standardized dress code. It limited her choices and eliminated most arguments when it was time for back-to-school shopping. But every time we had to buy clothing for a special occasion, we both knew a fight was bound to happen.

She would take forever to pick out clothes. Inevitably, I would lose my patience — and then the tears would flow. This year, we had prepared ourselves for the outing. We talked about what she wanted. She asked for a simple shirt, skirt and sandals. Once we got into the store and she saw all the options, the same frustrations built. She couldn't decide which skirt or shirt she wanted. In desperation, I whisper-yelled, "Why can't you just pick something?" Through tears, she cried back, "Because I don't know what I like. I never got the chance to figure it out."

Her words hit me hard. She was right. She never had the freedom to figure out what clothing she liked. When she was little, I bought her clothes without her. Once she started school, she wore uniforms. I did not give her space to determine what she liked or what fashion best suited her.

I swallowed my ego, which tasted pretty bitter, and took a deep breath. Then, I changed tactics by introducing fashion to her. I showed her the different prints on fabric and the various lengths and waists of skirts. It took another hour, but she finally decided on a purple t-shirt, a flowered skirt with an elastic waist, and neutral sandals. The next time my daughter needed a dress for a special occasion, I called my niece to take her shopping. My niece was patient and gave my daughter the space she needed to develop her fashion sense.

My daughter's first job was at a clothing boutique, where she developed a cool and casual style. She just needed the space and opportunity to do so. My guidelines are: Be comfortable and let your clothes honor who you are. If I am uncomfortable with her clothing, I ask myself why before approaching her. Usually, I feel this way when I worry other women will judge me.

Judgment has happened. Her senior year, she wore a short black dress to the homecoming dance. A woman in our community who did not have a daughter attending the dance made a social post expressing her disapproval of the girls' short dresses that she had seen posted. I spoke up and told her why I let my daughter leave the house in a short dress.

My daughter is confident, and  — to this one dance  — she wanted to wear a short dress. I remember typing, "Sometimes a short dress is just a short dress. A girl can wear a short dress and still have self-respect." Although there were some quiet "likes" to my response, the backlash was phenomenal. The louder voices informed me that boys react to what girls wear, and girls disrespect their bodies by showing them off. This is perplexing. Are they disrespecting their bodies when they wear shorts or swimsuits? We show much more skin in those outfits. But the accusation that my daughter's clothing choices could cause boys to lose their morality did me in. I said my piece in response to those allegations, and I logged off Facebook for three days. Parents, the idea that a girl's clothing makes boys act in a certain manner undermines the boy's self-control and places responsibility for other people's choices on an innocent girl. Please remember that this mindset originated in the 1800s and was used to shame girls. Let's change the conversation.

This conversation can be a befuddling one. Go with your gut, love and grace. If you make a wrong move, apologize. Tell her this is new territory for you as well. She will understand.

Ways to guide your daughter with her clothing and fashion choices:
• Watch how you talk about your body or the bodies of women; girls hear this
  talk and tend to internalize it, no matter whom you are talking about.
• Be careful how you talk about the size of clothing you wear; again, girls hear
  this talk and internalize it.
• Talk to her about what fashion is.
• Talk to her about your fashion choices.
• Take a trip to the store when there is no pressure to buy a specific outfit. Try letting
  your daughter take her time to look at and try on clothes.
• Encourage her to ask herself if she likes what she is wearing before asking others.
• Let her experiment with different clothing styles, colors and prints.
• If she wants to run errands with you while in a cowgirl outfit, princess dress,
  or in a plaid dress and glitter tights, let her.
• If you are uncomfortable with her choices, question yourself before questioning her.

If you are like me and have a daughter and a son, let him hear the fashion
conversation between you and your daughter. This way, he will understand why
girls may choose to wear or not wear specific clothing. Bring him in as an ally for
his sister and change the conversation about clothing and fashion. Of course,
there are fashion expectations for men as well. Perhaps hearing her fashion
conversation will help him with his fashion choices.

## LACE WITH GOLD EMBROIDERY
10 Fun & Slightly Crazy Facts About Clothing

- In the 1800s, people pinned live chameleons to their clothing as accessories or jewelry.
- According to Icelandic folklore, if you don't get new clothes to wear for Christmas, a Yule Cat will eat you (Gerstein, 2014).
- Until the 19th century, children were dressed as miniature adults.
- Until around 1910, it was common for little boys to wear dresses.
- During the 1860s, dresses were so wide that women often got stuck in doorways (Gerstein, 2014).
- The tiny pockets in jeans date back to the 1800s and were for cowboys to store their watches.
- The first pair of Levi's sold for $6 worth of gold dust (Gerstein, 2014).
- Blue once was considered a feminine color, while pink was a strong color for baby boys because it's a lighter form of red (Centeno, n.d.).
- The technical term for the end of a shoelace is an aglet.
- For characters depicted as being weird or offbeat, TV and movie costumes will outfit them in two clashing patterns (25 Random Fashion Facts You've Never Heard, n.d.).

## DESIGNERS REDESIGNING
Two Women Who Impacted the Clothing & Fashion Industry

Elizabeth Keckley was a seamstress and designer who worked her way out of slavery to become a successful dressmaker.

Born into slavery in 1818, Keckley became an accomplished seamstress by working to provide an income for the family that owned her. Eventually, she purchased her and her son's freedom. She became a dressmaker in Washington, D.C., attracting the attention of First Lady Mary Todd Lincoln, who made Keckley her personal dressmaker.

In her later years, Keckley taught other Black women how to become dressmakers so that they could earn incomes as well. Then, in 1892, she accepted a faculty position at Ohio's Wilberforce University. Keckley died in 1907 at age 89, leaving behind a legacy of rugged, selfless work that gave women purpose, beauty, and freedom (Elizabeth Keckly, n.d.).

Cuban-born designer, Isabel Toledo, honored self-expression through the art of needle and thread.

Born in 1960, Toledo's family emigrated to the United States when she was 8 years old. She learned to sew that same year. After high school, she attended the Fashion Institute of Technology before transferring to Parsons School of Design. However, she dropped out of Parsons when she was given an intern position at The Costume Institute of the Metropolitan Museum of Art (Phelps, 2019).

Toledo's work honors diversity. She designed clothes for First Lady Michelle Obama and established a clothing line for the fashion company Lane Bryant. She won multiple awards for her work but always remained humble in her craft. Toledo died in 2019. Her work inspired the design world by creating fashion honoring a woman's right to self-expression (Friedman, 2019).

*You are enough.*

*You.*
*Are.*
*Enough.*

# PERIODS & EXCLAMATION POINTS

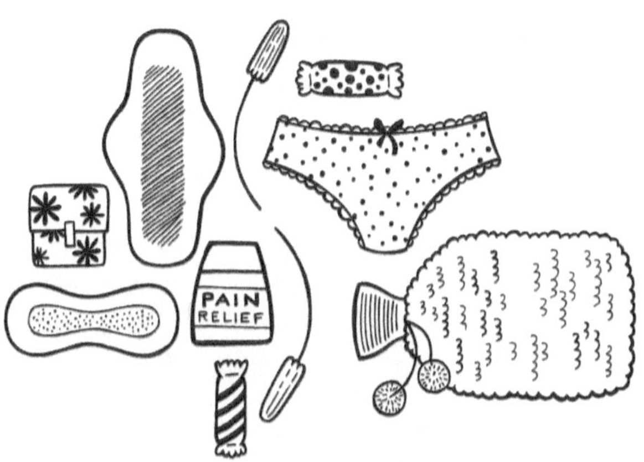



PERIOD:
A length of time; a small, dot-shaped punctuation mark that indicates the end of a sentence.

MENSTRUATION:
A regular discharge of blood and tissue from the lining of the uterus through the vagina.

VAGINA:
A muscular tunnel that connects the vulva to the neck of the uterus.

VULVA:
The outer part of the female genitals.

WHAT I'VE LEARNED:
It is not as alarming as it sounds, but it does feel like it should be called an exclamation point instead of a period.

# Chapter 6

Well, we are at The Chapter. I am not going to lie; this chapter has the potential to be pretty uncomfortable. We are going to talk about our periods. There is no way that I could write a book about beauty culture and not include a chapter about menstruation. I mean, it's something we all have in common, a shared experience. Like the bra chapter, this topic feels weird because we don't talk about it enough. For centuries, society has ignored women's menstruation, and now it feels taboo and has an embarrassing stigma. Girls never should be embarrassed about their cycles. If it wasn't for periods, there would be no humans. Menstruation = people. Period.

## MATTRESS PADS & THE BEACH
An Honest Confession of How I Didn't Suck Up All of the Water in the Ocean

I was 14 when I got my first period. I remember being anxious about how it would look and feel. It was like waiting for a jack-in-the-box to pop up. In some ways, I just wanted it to hurry up and happen. But, in other ways, I never wanted it to happen. I was nervous about the blood and what it would feel like. But, turns out my period took its time.

I was the last one in my group of friends to experience it. Month after month, my friends would gather around the lunch table, lean forward and, over soggy cafeteria nachos, share the deepest of secrets. Enthusiastically, they whispered, "I got it." At first, I responded, "Got what?" They would look at me, eyes wide, heads pushed forward, giving a slight "read between the lines" nod that only insiders understood. The rest of my friends gave an "OOOH" while I looked at everyone, late to the game, trying to figure out what it was. When I finally understood, I listened with morbid wonder and curiosity. I wanted to know how it started. I learned from their experiences. What they did and how they did it. One of my friends bravely told me how she got confused about which side of a pad went up. Unfortunately, she guessed wrong and stuck the sticky part on her ... self. I sat, wide-eyed, as she explained how she unstuck herself. I made a mental note: sticky side down.

Some of my friends voiced their experiences with tones that simultaneously bordered on pride and embarrassment. Some of them had no embarrassment at all. They looked forward to proudly wearing the menses' crown of attention. I wondered how I would share my news when it finally became my turn. As it turned out, I wouldn't get a chance to share. I had my first period during the summer before my freshman year in high school.

I was staying with my grandparents for the month and was utterly unprepared. I had almost forgotten that periods were a thing in the absence of friends. The next day, we would be on our way to visit my aunt in Myrtle Beach.

Twenty hours in a car, with my grandparents, and on my period?
No, thank you.

I was in a panic. I made a makeshift pad out of toilet paper (which didn't stay in place) and asked my grandma if I could call my mom. I told Mom, and she told me to put Grandma back on the phone so she could explain the situation. I went and hid in a back bedroom. I remember my grandma gently knocking on the bedroom door. She stuck her head in the room and, in a low voice, said, "Your mom told me you need some sanitary napkins." I wasn't sure what a sanitary napkin was, but then I saw she had some pads in her hand. She gave them to me and then went to the store for some more.

They were the biggest, thickest, bulkiest things I ever had seen. The size
alone made me worry about how much I would bleed. I mean, if the pad
had to be that thick, how much blood would come out of me? They were
so uncomfortable. There was no way I could walk normally with a big
mattress pad stuck to my underwear.

To my relief, the pads Grandma bought at the store were a little thinner
than the ones she had at her house. Also, it turns out that I didn't bleed that
much. However, three weeks later, I had it again. This time, I was in Myrtle
Beach, getting ready to go to the beach. How was I supposed to swim with a
pad? It would suck up all of the water in the ocean! This time, my aunt came
to the rescue. She introduced me to tampons and explained how to insert one —
and it was super-overwhelming at first. I went through at least five as I tried to
figure them out. I shed a few tears, but I figured it out and could enjoy the rest
of my time at the beach.

Managing my period at school was ... bumble-y. It was the one week every
month that I carried a purse with me. Taking your backpack to the bathroom
was a dead giveaway that you were on your period. But if you had a purse, you
could pretend you were going to fix your lip gloss or, in my case, clown makeup.
The guys caught on anyway, and they would make comments about me taking
my pads to the bathroom because Aunt Flo was visiting. I tried sticking the
tampon up my sleeve or in my pocket several times, but it fell out. That was
beyond embarrassing. All I could do was pick it up and act like it was no big
deal. Of course, it actually isn't a big deal — but, when you are a freshman
in high school, everything in life is a big deal.

I remember laughing through the "growing-up" classes in elementary and
middle school. One of my more annoying traits is that I laugh at the worst
times. If something is uncomfortable, my reaction is to laugh. The growing-up
class made me giggle uncontrollably to the point of tears. It all was so painfully
embarrassing. The teacher never laughed. She was always very serious, which
made me laugh even more. When we girls came back to class, the boys asked

us what we were doing, and we would say, "None of your beeswax" (which is old-school for "none of your business"). But somebody should have talked to the boys about menstruation. When you are 12 and don't understand something, it can make you feel uncomfortable. Often, we tease others to get away from those feelings, but that teasing comes at the cost of another's feelings. Getting made fun of for being on my period was humiliating. Ignoring the fact that all of the girls were leaving the classroom to talk about secret things never is a good idea. Instead, I wish a teacher would have taken the boys aside and said, "Look, if you want to be a dad someday, you will have to understand this thing called menstruation. You are here because a girl had her period. Never make fun of it!" Then maybe the pre-teen and teen years would have felt a little less bumble-y.

As an adult, this is the one area with which I struggle. I am comfortable asking my husband to buy tampons at the store, and I have taught my daughter to do the same. She also understands that she doesn't have to hide them from her brother. I am comfortable talking about periods with my girlfriends. But I still hide my tampons in the deep recesses of my bag. Speaking (or, in this case, writing) publicly about this subject makes me nervous. I was raised in a time when this type of talk was deemed inappropriate, and I have seen that mindset trickle down to the young girls in my self-esteem groups. They want to talk about periods, but are unsure how to bring it up to a group of girls who all will experience that same thing. Not being able to speak publicly about a natural, normal and shared experience feels wrong.

I hope that, by the end of this chapter, you will feel empowered enough to talk about your period. We are going to learn why we have periods. We will pry open the closed-minded beliefs that explain why people don't talk about them. We will uncover the history of menstruation products. Discovering the history of menstruation will help you feel comfortable and confident with your period. Maybe you won't giggle as much as I did in your "growing-up" classes. But, if you do, you are in good company.

Are you ready? Let's begin.

## QUESTION MARKS INSTEAD OF PERIODS
Understanding Menstruation

Menses, another name for a period, is what enables people to create life. It happens at the onset of puberty, anywhere from 10 to 16 years of age. The hormones that cause periods also can cause acne and weight gain. But, girls, weight gain during puberty is normal. Let me say it one more time, so the people in the back can hear:

**WEIGHT GAIN DURING PUBERTY IS NORMAL!**

Has anyone ever told you why you get a period? Of course, I'm talking about an explanation other than "so you can have babies." Has anyone actually explained what triggers your body into the menstruation cycle?

Not everybody understands why we have menstruation cycles. This is unfortunate because it is something many who are AFAB (assigned female at birth) experience. It happens to our bodies, so we need to understand this process. If we know the way our bodies work, we feel more comfortable with ourselves. When we are comfortable with our bodies, we are confident with our bodies.

If talking about your period makes you feel:
• Awkward
• Uncomfortable
• Wrong
• Silenced
then we are having the wrong conversation about periods. All girls should feel empowered to talk about their periods — without shame or stigma.

*Sweet Girl,*

*Girls never should feel intimidated or embarrassed to talk about their bodies, especially in regard to something we have no control over. Never refrain from asking questions that will help you understand yourself simply to make someone else comfortable. Keep working to understand your body so you will know how to take care of it. You are so important. I urge you to take the time to understand how menstruation works. Understanding these things will help you make the best-informed decisions for your mind, body and spirit. Don't let the world decide for you. You are in charge of you.*

We are going to start our journey by learning why girls have periods. This process is very much like watching dominoes fall. They all work together to produce a result. I am not a doctor or a scientist, just a woman working to understand her body so I can help you know yours. So, here we go.

There is a small gland in your brain called the pituitary gland. This gland is responsible for growth. It emits hormones that tell your body how to develop. As your body grows from child to teen and eventually adult, your hips widen, your thighs look more like a teenager's, and your breasts develop. This is how our bodies are biologically programmed to grow. The growth in these areas produces gynoid or reproductive fat. (Deep breath, "fat" is not a bad word. As an adult, if you decide to have a baby, it provides nourishment for him or her. Fat can be good. Ready to continue? Okay.) After a while, this fat releases chemicals that trigger the pituitary gland to release a hormone called leptin. Leptin has an important job (Blaffer Hrdy, 1999).

Leptin signals cause another chemical called gonadotropin to get to work. Gonadotropin signals the ovaries to get ready to release an egg. (An egg is the female reproductive cell of animals and plants.) This whole delicate process happens again and again as you enter puberty. Eventually, this process will cause your ovaries to release an egg. The egg travels to your uterus, prompting your uterus walls to thicken with extra tissue — blood and fluid — if you get pregnant. The egg will attach itself to this extra padding. If you are not pregnant, the egg doesn't need to attach itself to anything, and you don't need this extra lining. It breaks down and expels itself through your vagina and out the vulva. That is the discharge of a period cycle. The discharge can be a slow trickle of blood, or it can be thicker. Sometimes there is cramping, caused by muscles contracting to expel the blood and tissue. There are pain relievers for any discomfort you may feel. When a woman is pregnant she typically does not have a period, as the body keeps the extra tissue. Historically, the absence of a period has been used as an indicator of pregnancy. There are some people assigned female at birth who do not experience periods for a variety of reasons. If you do not experience your period, take a deep breath and talk to a parent, trusted adult, school counselor or nurse about your concern. There are a variety of reasons why you may be experiencing this. A doctor will be able to help you.

There is one aspect of menstruation that can be befuddling. Hormones. While on your period, you can feel very emotional. This is something that many girls have experienced. One moment you are fine, and then the next, you feel sad, angry, or just annoyed. There are a lot of hormones released during the menstruation cycle. Hormones are basically different chemicals produced by the cells in your body. Hormones might affect your emotions, make you tired, cause headaches, weight gain, or make you bloated (meaning your body holds fluid or gas, which causes a minor and temporary distended feeling to your stomach area). When you feel sad or anxious and can't figure out why, remember those sneaky hormones and that it's normal to feel emotional during your period. You are not crazy. One last note on hormones: Those pesky things also can cause acne. Acne is part of puberty. It won't last forever, and there are many products to get rid of it. Don't get discouraged. Almost everyone has to deal with acne. It is hard, but it is manageable and it will pass.

Just to be clear, your period actually is a cycle. This cycle lasts around 28 days, with the bleeding marking its conclusion — just like a period at the end of a sentence. You bleed for a few days or up to a week. At first, it can feel overwhelming, awful, confusing and gross. After some time, you realize how manageable it really is. It isn't fun, but it is figure-out-able. It is even more manageable when you talk about it with your parents: both of them if you can, not just your mom. Dads need to be involved. Maybe your dad doesn't need to be there for all of the details — I know that can be awkward — but, if you need help, he will want to be there for you. Your dad was born because his mom had a period. Being a dad also means helping a daughter understand and manage her period.

Side note: There are times when your body, for one reason or another, works differently than other girls' bodies. If you think something is off about your period, speak up. Better to speak up and be wrong than stay silent and be right. This may make you feel nervous, and you can counter that nervousness with an honest conversation with your parents or another trusted adult.

## Moon Goddesses & Temples
### Menstruation in Ancient Civilizations

Now that we understand what menstruation is and how it works, let's dive into the history of period care. Documentation of it is a little dotty. Men are the recorders of history. However, menstruation wasn't talked about — and, since men never experienced menstruation, it's not recorded in great detail. I am not sure how men decided what to write since it was something they knew nothing about. No one really understood what menstruation was or why it happened. Doctors formed theories based on what little they understood of the human body. But, as we soon shall see, most of them were wildly inaccurate. Many of the beliefs were based on the theory that menstruation occurred in women because they were the weaker gender.

Unfortunately, these beliefs embarrassed and shamed many women. As a result, people made unwise decisions based on faulty information. One unwise and erroneous assumption was that a girl's first period was her transition from child to woman. In ancient civilizations, it was (and many times still is) believed a girl's menses meant she was ready to be married and start a family. While a girl's first period is a milestone, it is not the moment she turns into a woman. There is plenty of childhood on the other side of a girl's first period.

People knew periods had to do with a woman's ability to have a baby, but they weren't sure how or why. Think about it: Nobody knew what the inside of a human looked like, much less how our bodies functioned. Doctors had to guess what was going on inside of us. Many studied cadavers to get an idea. However, those bodies didn't give insight into how a living body worked. Furthermore, they had no knowledge of cells, or ways to see those microscopic parts that make our bodies work correctly. Doctors did the best they could and formed theories and ideas based on their limited knowledge and beliefs of the time. As we get further into the chapter, you will notice how beliefs around menstruation changed. This gets pretty confusing for women. Men were deciding for them about an issue that they never had experienced. However, once women were given the space to contribute to the study of menstruation, they could solve their own period issues pretty effectively.

In ancient times, blood represented life. However, the act of bleeding was associated with death. I think this made the idea of menstruation complicated. Anthropologists translated hieroglyphics to understand ancient Egyptian beliefs about menstruation or what they called hsmn. Egyptians referred to a woman on her period as a bleeding woman (Frandsen, 2007). They believed menses blood, fertility and the moon were associated with each other. People prayed to the moon goddess when they wanted to have a family. However, they also believed in another god who disliked bleeding women, and they could not enter his temple. This is one of the first times menses is considered taboo. In fact, the word "taboo" is translated from the mention of this god and his temple (Habiger, 1998).

There is evidence that women separated from society during their periods. The period process was called purification. The woman's body was purifying itself of unwanted blood. It was believed that women had extra blood because they were "wetter" than men. It was thought that all openings on a woman's body (nostrils, ears, mouth, etc.) led to the vulva. Therefore, the theory was that excess liquid would leave their bodies once a month. The woman was able to rejoin the village when her period was over. They believed that women ceased to bleed during pregnancy because the blood was rerouted to the baby and used for nourishment.

To manage the blood, women had two choices: Use something to absorb the blood inside the body or as it seeped from the body. Women used rudimentary tampons (inserted through the vulva into the vagina, which absorbed blood inside the body) made of papyrus or pads made of fabric. But the pads (which absorbed blood once it came out of the vulva) would have to be washed and reused again and again. Also, since the blood was considered impure, no one wanted to be the person who laundered them. All that being said, there is evidence that period blood was believed to have some healing properties. For example, it was used to make ointments to heal leprosy, sagging breasts and headaches (Habiger, 1998).

Practices in ancient Greece and Rome were similar to those used in Egypt. They believed women experienced menstruation because their bodies were spongy and absorbed moisture from the air. They stored this moisture in the womb. Men did not absorb as much moisture because they were more active than women (Schroeder, 1976). Therefore, blood from menstruation could destroy crops and sour wine. Documentation suggests that Greek and Roman women managed their flow using pads or tampons made from soft wood or plant fibers wrapped in linen.

During this time, people noticed the emotions women experienced around their periods. (Remember when we talked about how people developed theories based on what they thought was true? Keep that in mind as we walk through this next little section.)

People believed the uterus was where excess fluid was stored, and babies were formed and carried. Doctors thought it was the most critical organ in the female body, even more important than a woman's brain. They also believed a woman was emotional because the uterus wandered around her body, causing discomfort. Except doctors didn't use the word "emotional" but, rather, "hysterical." The uterus could be lured back into its proper place by smelling salts or sneezing. As crazy as this theory sounds, it would follow women throughout the centuries. It also was why many people thought women were fragile — and why they weren't taken seriously when they were upset about something. Their wandering uteruses made them hysterical. Sigh.

In Egypt, Greece and Rome, women used plants, herbs and oils to ease the pain or discomfort of menstruation. Women supported and helped each other out during this time of the month. Women are exceptional at being each other's support systems. However, as we enter the Middle Ages, we will see how religion changed the views of menstruation and women's ability to help each other out.

## Toad-al Hysteria

Menses Through the Middle Ages & Victorian Era

In the Middle Ages, things really got confusing. Again, blood was both good and bad — life and death. Men, who never had experienced a period, still were telling women why they had menses and how they should handle the situation. Science was very much tied to religion. The Catholic church had a lot of money and could easily influence those in power. Therefore, countries followed the doctrines passed down by the church. If you wanted to go to Heaven, you did what that church said to do. So when the church said that women on their periods needed no relief from pain, nobody offered help. The leading men of the Catholic church believed periods were the curse God spoke of after Eve's little apple fiasco in the Garden of Eden. There was no pain relief because menstruation was the curse women brought upon themselves when Eve ate the apple. Therefore, if a woman had period pain, she had to suffer through it as her penance for this sin. I am not sure about that logic. Why did one woman's actions have to affect all women? Nevertheless, that's what the church dictated. However, it was believed that women could get pain relief upon digesting the ashes of a toad. So, you know, suffer through cramps or eat a toad — your choice.

Women would manage their discharge by wearing rags or pads between their legs. They made the pad out of bits of cotton, itchy wool or an absorbent moss layered between the fabric. It helped that women wore so many layers of clothing. If the rag or moss pad leaked, then the layers of material could absorb the blood, and no one would notice the leak. These pads were not disposable and needed to be washed and reused throughout the cycle. Daily baths were not a common practice during the Middle Ages. Smells from period blood and the constant use of fabric rags and pads were natural but not very pleasant. Women carried incense and flowers to hide the smell and avoid shame.

Medical science took shape during the 1800s. Doctors worked to understand how human bodies operated and established theories on observable science rather than religion. But, this doesn't mean things were better for women. They still weren't recognized as man's equal or thought of as intellectual. As a result, women were doubted and, at times, considered hysterical.

People believed the all-important uterus needed care and protection. Doctors thought that most illnesses women experienced resulted from the uterus not being able to bleed sufficiently during menses. Girls and women were told to rest during their periods. They weren't supposed to physically or mentally exert themselves. If they did, it could make them insane or damage their uterus. Fertility was a girl's keystone. Getting married and creating a family was her purpose.

Since people believed the feminine body was not as mentally, emotionally or physically strong as a male's, steps were taken to lower the stress levels of girls and women. This meant education was less rigorous. Girls didn't learn as much math and science as boys because those subjects were exacting and would hurt a girl's brain and uterus. (Plus, people didn't think math and science were necessary to raise a family.)

The constant housework and family responsibilities meant very few women could rest for several days while on their periods. Those who could typically were wealthy and had servants who could carry on with the daily responsibilities of managing a home. However, women who had to work avoided things that doctors believed could damage a woman's blood flow. For example, doctors thought if a woman became chilled during her period, her blood flow could stop. As a result, women would avoid getting cold during that time of the month (That Time of the Month in Victorian England, 2017).

Women refrained from speaking about their menstruation. Society considered it offensive to talk about or indicate that one was on her period. Unfortunately, this led to very little explanation for young girls about reproduction and menstruation. This silence led to misinformation, confusion and sometimes fear.

A Baltic German naturalist and embryologist named Karl Ernst von Baer discovered the purpose of ovaries in 1827. Although there still was much to learn, medical professionals started understanding why women bled each month. But this meant society now believed the ovaries, not the uterus, were the most crucial part of a woman's body. However, there finally was some compassion for women during their monthly "predicament." People finally realized women needed sound medical advice to guide them through menstruation (Dupont, 2008).

In the late 1800s, a British surgeon and medical scientist named Dr. Joseph Lister would become known as the "Father of Antiseptic Surgery" when he discovered how to prevent infection in wounds during and after surgery. Lister's work, in turn, inspired a medicated plaster maker (Robert Wood Johnson) to team up with his brothers in 1886 and create Johnson &

Johnson — the first business to mass-produce sterile surgical dressings and sutures. In 1897, Johnson & Johnson introduced the first disposable sanitary napkin, appropriately dubbed Lister's Pads.

Disposable pads were revolutionary as they made personal care more manageable and less messy. Until this point, women wore cloth rags or let their many layers of clothing absorb their blood. Women kept pads in place with sanitary belts that fit around the waist with a strap between the legs. The pad was fastened to the strap and was very uncomfortable. Women wore period bloomers and underwear that worked much like a rubber diaper. However, these undergarments didn't allow the skin to breathe, which caused sweat, heat and more unpleasant odors (Gabillet, 2018).

## SANITARY FREEDOM
How Women Took Charge of Their Periods in the U.S.

Much like everything else in this book, the 20th century brings about changes and freedom for women. As women's fashion changed, so did the need for period protection. If a woman leaked through a pad or rag while she was wearing a hoop skirt or several petticoats, it was doubtful the stain would soak all the way through to her outer skirts. However, as fabric became light and thin, women on their periods had to take extra care so that their pads would not leak through their dresses and also that people would not be able to see their sanitary belts.

During World War I, nurses discovered that cellulose gel pads (made of cotton, flax or other plant fibers) did a better job of absorbing the blood of wounded soldiers. These nurses started using the gel pads for their own menstruating purposes. A company called Kotex heard about the discovery and, in 1918, made the first period pad with cellulose gel. As a result, women could go

longer between changing their pads without worrying about leakage.
(To these nurses, I give a huge salute!)

Talking about periods still was considered impolite, and shop owners realized some women might feel embarrassed to buy pads, especially from a male shopkeeper. So they started placing a locked money box next to the pads on store shelves. Women slipped money into the box, took the pads, and never had to talk to anyone in the store. While this was nice, it reinforced the silent taboo surrounding menstruation.

By 1927, multiple companies made period protection for women, and the personal-care industry was a thriving business. As a result, the negative stigma associated with menstruation started to lift but never would go away completely (Gabillet, 2018).

The 1930s saw several advances in the personal-care industry. An American actor, inventor and author named Leona Chalmers invented the menstrual cup. The small rubber cup was inserted into the vulva to catch the blood. However, women did not like it because it was heavy, hard and challenging to put in and take out. However, in 1936, a product hit the market that freed women from the discomforts of their period like never before.

Noticing the embarrassment his wife and patients experienced with period care, Dr. Earle Haas designed a modern-day tampon (designed like a plug) made of cotton encased in an applicator. The applicator allowed a woman to smoothly insert the tampon and push it into place while keeping her fingers free of blood. The doctor tried marketing his invention to other entities, including Johnson & Johnson, with no substantial interest. A Colorado businesswoman named Gertrude Voss Tendrich (who would found Tampax and become its first president) purchased the doctor's patent in 1933 for $32,000. She spent the next few years hiring women to work on the design and men to get the product into stores.

At first, stores were resistant to selling tampons. Some people shunned the thought of inserting anything into the vulva, labeling it improper and immoral. It wasn't until women understood how they worked and the freedom that came from wearing one that they began selling. Women slowly were claiming independence from their periods, and ovaries no longer were considered the most important part of the female body. During this same time, women were entering the workforce and being allowed to advance their education. Finally, the pain reliever, Midol, started specifically advertising for period pain.

For those wary of using a tampon, another woman inventor was busy designing a less-cumbersome belt that would hold pads in place. Mary Beatrice Kenner invented a sanitary belt that held the disposable pad in place with an adhesive. This meant women no longer had to worry about pinning pads in place. Instead, the adhesive strip secured it in place. However, Kenner couldn't afford a patent for the belt until the 1950s. When she finally did patent it, a company contacted her to offer her a marketing deal. However, they backed out when they realized Kenner was Black (Mallasasime, 2021).

Even with these advancements, society still shunned period talk. Instead, pamphlets were made for mothers to give to their daughters so they could understand what menstruation was. The printed word took the place of verbal explanation. This silence made periods feel mysterious. Ads for personal care shamed girls into taking care of themselves during this time of the month, warning them that if there was a smell, boys would be repelled — and girls no longer would be considered dainty or ladylike. These condescending ads convinced women that silence was best and that they never should let anyone know it was "that time of the month."

Self-adhesive pads were developed in the '60s. Women no longer needed a sanitary belt to hold a pad in place. Now the pad stuck to the underwear. Personal-care ads were placed in women's magazines but were not allowed on TV until 1972. When they did air, people objected. Since no one talked openly about their periods, a televised ad for personal care was shocking. Actors couldn't say "period" and "blood" in the commercial; instead, the actor told women to read about the tampon in magazine ads. In reality, all the TV commercials did was refer women back to the printed word. It wasn't until 1985 that a commercial actually used the word "period."

In the '70s, two books hit the market that opened the doors for girls and women to lift the stigma surrounding period talk. "Are You There God? It's Me, Margaret." is a fictional book about a girl going through puberty. It puts a humorous spin on a confusing time. The nonfiction book "Our Bodies, Ourselves" created space for books like "Her Story."

"Our Bodies, Ourselves" explained and normalized the female body, giving girls a sense of pride in how their bodies worked. It described bodies as something to love, talk about and celebrate. By 1980, "female hysteria" finally was removed from medical diagnostic books.

Today, women still are working on lifting the stigma surrounding period talk and practices. Menstruation cups have improved and now are available to purchase in the same aisle as pads and tampons. There also are period panties and swimsuits that offer alternatives to pads and tampons. However, discomfort still surrounds the topic because the conversation is new. Period education is severely lacking in our country and in countries where women are secondary citizens. There are places where entire cultures still believe women on their periods can poison food, water and crops. Some girls do not have access to period protection and can't attend school because they could experience leakage through their clothing. They miss several days of school once a month, which adds up. Fortunately, there are programs and people who work tirelessly to bring period education and protection to these countries. No girl should feel trapped and controlled by her period because periods = people. Exclamation point.

## A FUNNY TWIST OF FATE
Embracing the Truth

The truth is, your body is incredible. It is built just for you, to get you everywhere you need to go in life. Whether you want to have children or want to marry, it is built for you to accomplish whatever goals you set for yourself. You should be able to feel comfortable with it, talk about it, celebrate it, laugh about it, love it and honor it. You should be able to manage your period in whatever manner you wish. Never feel embarrassed or stifled by expressing your feelings and concerns about menses.

*Sweet Girl,*
*The most important thing you can do for yourself is to learn how to be comfortable in your own body. Learn how it works, learn how to take care of it, learn how to talk about it and never be ashamed of it. Your body is enough.*

*Your body is enough.*

*You.*

*Are.*

*Enough.*

*When it is time for you to manage your period, remember:*
- *Talk to your parents.*
- *Read up on different period protection and experiment with the items to determine what you're most comfortable using.*
- *If you are uncomfortable with something, find a trusted person with whom you can speak candidly.*
- *It's normal to feel awkward when you are learning to manage your period.*
- *Never compare yourself to others; everyone's body and journey is unique.*
- *Understand the parts of your body that are involved in menstruation. They are not just for having babies; they are the parts that help make up the wonder of you.*

Parents,

Guiding your daughter through her first few periods can feel overwhelming.
Be proactive in your conversations with her. Explain all of the options for period
care and then follow her lead as she determines what is best for her. This will help
her feel comfortable with her period and her body. With comfort comes confidence.

I talked to my daughter about reproduction when she was 10. I remember we were
driving in the car. She was belted to the seat and couldn't go anywhere, and we
had the whole talk. I talked about all of it. From eggs and ovaries to vulva and vagina.
She needed to understand what their purpose was and how they worked. I decided
that if I only talked about periods and left the rest of the information out, I was
shrouding things in mystery. I wanted to talk to her before someone at school
did. I didn't want any misinformation making its way to her.

I giggled through our talk. My husband was calmer about it, but I was awkward
and unpolished. She wouldn't make eye contact with us. But we got through it.
Then, she asked that we never speak about vaginas again, "too many Vs" —
which made me nervous-laugh even harder.

In a crazy twist of fate, my daughter had her first period at her grandmother's house.
It was, literally, the same experience as mine. I got a tearful telephone call from
her, spoke to her grandma, and Grandma went to the store for pads. I already had
stocked her bathroom with pads and tampons; I just didn't think to send anything
with her to Grandma's house. I explained how both products worked and told her
she had the right to decide what was best for her. She quickly learned how to
tell her father and me what products she wanted/needed from the store.

When talking with your daughter about her period, please consider
the following:
• What do you wish you would have known about menstruation when you
  were her age?
• Are you comfortable with her using tampons, cups, or purchasing period panties?

- Discuss Toxic Shock Syndrome.
- How do you feel about periods?
- Are you comfortable talking about menstruation? Why or why not?
- It is important to watch how you refer to periods; negative connotations can cause thoughts and feelings of embarrassment and shame.
- What does "menses" mean to you?
- Be prepared with products for periods, acne and cramps.
- Dads, what education do you need to help your daughter understand menstruation?

This is where I usually say, "If you have a boy, let him hear the conversation between you and your daughter." I approached this topic a bit differently. My children have a pretty big age gap between them. So, instead, I took my son with me when I bought tampons. I even have discussed being on my period and having cramps or headaches. It sounds like, "I am not feeling like myself today. I think it is because I am on my period." He can attempt to understand what his sister and other girls are experiencing from this. I am not sure if she ever has said anything to him about it, but she doesn't feel like she needs to hide her products from him. Finally, when he was 10, he got his puberty talk, and I explained periods. He asked if that was why girls used tampons and where they went. Through giggles (yet again), I told him. He was embarrassed, but we got through it. It is life and, should he decide to be a father, he will need to understand that periods = people!

## EXCLAMATION POINT
10 Fun & Slightly Crazy Facts About Periods

- Don't worry about staining your underwear; most women have period stains on their underwear.
- The average woman has 450 periods in her lifetime.
- The average number of tampons used in a cycle is 18; thus, they often are sold in boxes of 18 or 36.

- All women go through menopause, which signifies the time when they no longer have a period. This process usually happens when a woman is in her late 40s or early 50s.
- The first actor to say "period" on TV was Courteney Cox, back in 1985. In later years, she would play Monica on the TV show "Friends."
- The female egg is the largest cell in the feminine body.
- Nicknames for the period include: "Aunt Flow" (also "Aunt Flo"), "On the Rag" and "Monthly Visitor."
- In Latin, menstruation means "monthly."
- The word tampon is French for "plug."

## DESTIGMATIZING OUR FLOWS
Embracing Menstruation

Businesswoman Gertrude Tendrich forever changed period care for women.

In 1933, Gertrude Tendrich purchased the patent for tampons from Dr. Earle Haas. The tampon looked like a compressed cotton plug with an attached string inside a paper tube. Tendrich purchased the patent for $32,000. She envisioned an all-woman business to help women manage their periods. At first, she hand-sewed the tampons herself. Eventually, she scaled up, and in 1936 her company, Tampax, hit the market with a magazine ad welcoming women to celebrate "a new day for womanhood" with "sanitary protection worn internally."

Ten years later, Tampax was in the education business. "Tampax Ladies" traveled to schools and colleges to educate people on their products. Tampax remains in business today and has a global reach. Tendrich's vision freed women from uncomfortable menstruation care and lifted period shame by giving us words to talk about a shared biological experience.

The Pad Project is committed to destigmatizing periods for women and menstruators worldwide.

In certain parts of the world, menstruation continues to be misunderstood and, in many places, girls and women can't access period care. In 2018, a documentary was filmed about period stigmas in India. This film, "Period. End of Sentence.," grew into a business that helps supply pad machines to rural communities in countries where menstruation education and care are much needed. The Pad Project also works in the U.S. to help those who menstruate get the period care they need despite their financial abilities. The Pad Project is making period care accessible to all.

*You are enough.*

*You.*
*Are.*
*Enough.*

# THE LIFT OF A FRIEND

FRIEND:

A person attached to another by feelings of affection.

WHAT I'VE LEARNED:

All acquaintances are not friends; one must never be in a rush
to find the perfect friend. When the time is right, she will be there.

Chapter 7

## CHAI WITH BRAIDS

An Honest Confession of Friendship Observed

I was in India, sitting in the library of a home for girls. I was a volunteer, helping the girls process traumas they had lived through. I watched as the three Indian women talked with each other. We were on our afternoon tea break, which quickly became my favorite part of the day. The door would open, and the cook would bring in a tray of the most delicious chai I had ever tasted. The girls participating in the program were dismissed to go to the kitchen to get a snack. We as volunteers would gather, drink chai, talk and check our emails. Our female translators always gathered and talked intimately amongst themselves. They enamored me with their intimacy. They gracefully invaded each other's personal space until there was none. Absent-mindedly, they played with each other's hair, picked fuzz off their saris, and gave each other massages while laughing and talking in Hindi. I felt like I was watching a secret symphony of friendship. I wasn't sure how well they knew one another, but their physical contact led me to believe they had a history. But then I realized I was putting my American spin on their friendship.

My best friend and I met in the seventh grade. We now live a state apart but still communicate every day, sometimes several times a day. When we are together, which averages 2-3 times a year (not nearly as much as we would like), I don't think I ever have reached over and started braiding her hair. However, these ladies were gently playing with each other's hair as they laughed and talked in low voices. Perhaps that is just how they are, so loving

and open to friendships that they immediately embraced one another without
hesitation. Their movements were accepting, empathetic and vulnerable —
exactly what friendship should be.

If one thing has helped get me through life, it's my friendships. Of course,
I have close guy friends I always will treasure. However, this chapter is all about
my female friendships. I tend to be a bit of a loner. I have eaten at restaurants
by myself and purposely stayed home when others were out together. But, for
my biggest celebrations and heartaches, I have wanted my girlfriends with me.
There has been someone to help me laugh at every stage in my life. I have
forever etched their names in my heart, all linked to specific times and places.
Even if I don't see them anymore, thanks to social media, I still get glimpses
into their lives and see the women they have become.

I have my group of girlfriends whom I rely on and who rely on me. Friends
must both give and receive in order for friendships to work. There are friends
from whom I have walked away, and I am sure some people have distanced
themselves from me. Not everyone will like you; it is a painful fact, but it doesn't
make you any less of a person. The older I get, the smaller my circle of friends
has become. This is how life works. You get wiser with age. You learn whom you
can depend on and whom you want to depend on you. You get to decide who
deserves your time and who doesn't.

My closest friends are the people who accept me for who I am. I never pretend
to like the same things they do, and they don't expect me to. In fact, there are
some women whom I treasure dearly, and we have completely opposite views
on politics and religion. It makes the friendship more meaningful because
it means we truly belong together. My best friend and I are incredibly similar.
We had some bumpy starts to our relationship, but we were very committed
to each other and worked them out. I can't imagine my life without her.

As an adult, the value of friendship is priceless. Having people who understand
and "get" you is a breath of fresh air. It's nice to be surrounded by women who

will challenge me to be my best self. They make me want to be a better person.
I think that is the foundation of all relationships. Women who want the best
for each other form the strongest, most resilient friendships. They can —
and will — get each other through pretty much anything.

## HOLDING HANDS & WALKING AWAY
The Life Cycle of Friendships

Friendships are a huge part of our culture. They start in our childhood.
Remember when you were in kindergarten? Life was simple, and it was so easy
to be friends with other girls. You played together at recess, perhaps holding
hands as you ran around the playground. At learning centers, you built things
together, made art, or played in the home living area. At lunch, you giggled
as you ate your turkey sandwiches. It's simple to be friends with someone
when you are 5.

As you get older, friendships can get confusing, but they level back out again.
One year, you are best friends with Sally, and the next year she may completely
ignore you. I was in my 30s when I solidified my friendships. That is really the
only way to put it. When I figured out who I was, I understood who I wanted
to be around. My friendships lasted longer; they were solid. I think that is
why relationships change so much when we are young. We don't know who
we are or what we want out of life, so how are we supposed to know with
whom we want to be friends?

It's important to remember that everyone is trying to figure life out. If someone
stops being friends with you, it is probably more about them and less about
you. Unless, of course, your actions hurt them. In that case, make your
amends and move on. Sometimes, you are friends with a person for a
short time. The relationship has a specific purpose, and then it's gone.

If you feel that being friends means:
• Fitting in with those around you
• Changing your likes to suit other people
• Giving more to the relationship than others do
• Jealousy, drama and gossip
• Hanging around people who make you feel uncomfortable
• Feeling bad about yourself
then we need to change the conversation. Your friendships should empower you, not cause self-doubt.

*Sweet Reader,*
*You deserve to be friends with those who see your value. You are worthy of a solid friendship. Whether you have that now or still are searching, make sure your friends honor your spirit — and you do the same. Never feel pressured to change who you are to please someone else. Be aware of those who are constantly needy. Someone who always is needing your aid and attention is not a friend. Friendships must be equal in all ways. Starting a friendship on uneven ground is a guarantee of pain and tears to come. You were made to be you, and your best friend is waiting to meet you. You are enough.*

*You are enough.*

*You.*
*Are.*
*Enough.*

When girls unite, they form a strong and powerful bond that lifts them and others up. In this chapter, you will read about historic friendships that empowered others. Several relationships we will talk about had such a strong lift that their impact has lasted centuries! Parts of this chapter will jump back and forth through time to talk about that impact. My goal is for you to understand how powerful friendships can be. Female friendships have a pretty fun history. Learning how vital they are to our world will help you know how important it is for you to have relationships that lift and support you.

Side Note: I did not include a section at the end of this chapter that highlights women entrepreneurs. Instead, I threaded the whole chapter with women who have bonded and used their friendships to give a lift to the world. After all, friends should bring out the best in us. It should nurture us to the point that we want to share that nurturing vibe with the rest of the world.

Are you ready? Let's begin.

## GOSSIPS & LIFELINES
### The Power of Friendships

The world's first friendships formed in prehistoric societies when people banded together to gather food and for safety. Evidence suggests that women began the first specific vocal communication that developed into language. This communication is called motherese. I think this is a pretty cool fact, since relationships are based on the ability to communicate effectively with each other.

Aristotle, a philosopher from ancient Greece, said the truest friends are two people who are bonded together by mutual affection. They care deeply about the well-being of one another. Relationships not built on these foundations will dissolve (Yalom, Brown, 2015). I have to agree with him 100%. But, of course, Aristotle also said women did not have the intelligence to manage such a friendship. So on this, I disagree with him 100%.

Women have been caring for each other for centuries. Through their relationships, nonprofits were created, aid was given to those in need, wars were won and laws were changed. By herself, a woman is a powerhouse; when united, women are unstoppable.

Of course, women in ancient civilizations had a more challenging time establishing relationships. They always were at home, tending to the house

and family. If they had to work for a living, that took up most of their time.
This was compounded by the fact that women simply did not have the freedom
to move about their communities and make their own decisions like men did.
As a result, a woman's friends were typically family members: mothers, sisters,
aunts and cousins (all of whom make the dearest of friends, as I have no idea
where I would be without my mom or sister).

During the Middle Ages, nuns exemplified some of the first documented
female friendships. They would write about each other in their letters and
personal journal entries. They described how their friends looked and their
personalities (Yalom, Brown, 2015). In their letters to each other, they
encouraged one another to pray, fast and work on being better versions
of themselves. They also showed support for each other's endeavors and
accomplishments.

The word "gossip" has existed in some form since the early 1000s —
originating from the Middle English "gossib" or "godsib(be)," meaning
"godparent" — but, in the 1500s, it transformed into a term used to describe
a woman's confidante. (Today, as you know, the word has a negative meaning.)
In the 16th century, friendships usually developed between women of the same
social class. Women were each other's fiercest allies. For example, when Queen
Elizabeth I contracted smallpox and was on the verge of death, her closest
confidante, Lady Mary Dudley Sidney, nursed her back to health. Unfortunately,
Mary ended up with smallpox as well and the disease left her horribly scarred.
(While I do not condone putting yourself at risk for a friend, this is an
example of how much women care for one another.)

A century later, on a small island in the Korea Strait, a group of women took
over an industry that would forever change life on their island. Though nobody
is quite sure how long the inhabitants of Jeju Island have made a living from
harvesting shellfish from the ocean floor, archaeologists have found evidence
that potentially traces the activity as far back as 300 B.C.E. In the 1600s, women
took over diving for reasons no one is quite sure about. Many historians believe

women assumed the role because men had left the island to fight in various wars. Or perhaps it was because there isn't a tax on a woman's income. Whatever the reason, the hænyeo way of life was born. This lifestyle exists to this day. The all-women divers harvest shellfish and sustain the delicate aquatic ecosystem around them.

The women work together and provide a way of life for their community. The island is built on volcanic rock, which means there is little naturally grown food. Shellfish are a mainstay of their diet and income. The hænyeo are world-renowned. Their unique way of life brings tourists to the island, which opens up another source of income. These women have worked together to serve and preserve their way of life for more than 400 years (Cataneo, 2017).

In the mid-1600s, The Friendship Society was established in England. The Society, made up of women (and a few men), met to discuss art and literature. This group would serve as a model for friendly gatherings among women for centuries and in many countries. In addition, it gave birth to many of the life-changing organizations that helped people through the toughest of times, which you will read about later on in this chapter (Yalom and Brown, 2015).

In the 18th century, a wealthy woman named Elizabeth Montagu started another friendship group called The Blue Stockings Society. She brought together women who desired intelligent conversation about the current state of affairs in Europe. Remember, women were considered fragile and not as intellectual as men, so they were denied a rigorous education. This friendship gave women the means for stimulating conversation that otherwise wouldn't have been available to them. In fact, many prominent members of English society joined the group. Elizabeth's Blue Stockings Society was an anomaly. It was a literary society, started for women by a woman who had inherited her husband's fortune. This simply wasn't the norm in 18th-century England (Chopra, n.d.).

Working-class women formed friendships that eased the demands of life. These friendships were vital, as women could support and help each other out. Working-class women had to balance childcare, household duties and physically demanding jobs. Knowing there would be a friend to help you out — listening when you needed someone to talk to, or laughing with you when there was joy — was, and still is, an essential need for everyone.

In the United States, women's friendships developed based on proximity and social class. Wealthy women gathered to discuss their husbands' jobs and fashion, as well as to commiserate. They shared practical living advice on child-rearing as well as household and servant management. However, working-class women helped one another out with basic needs, like childcare and emotional support. Friends were a critical lifeline. Knowing there was someone out there who understood you made life more enjoyable.

These lifelines were vital, because it was the woman whose life drastically changed when she married. She was the one who had to leave her home to follow and support her husband. As a result, neighbors would become a support system — especially during the early years of marriage, pregnancy and childbirth. Women didn't always have their mothers or sisters to lean on during those hard times; hence, female neighbors became their closest confidants.

Women's friendships became a mainstay of American culture. A consciousness rose from these groups, as often happens when women gather. A want to serve each other, lend a hand or provide a solution became the mission for many friendships. As mentioned earlier, working-class women didn't always have the time or freedom to gather like wealthier women. However, many realized they could do their work while visiting with friends. Women would bring their sewing with them while visiting friends. This was the start of knitting circles and quilting bees. Quilts were a universal need for all families. Women would gather and bring their bits of material, contributing or trading with each other as they made bedding for their families. Often the women would share a meal as they helped each other sew. For enslaved women, coming together to make quilts was a way of preserving their tradition and heritage. It also provided connection and support during a time when they were in constant fear of their and their family's lives.

A quilting-bee tradition, born out of a friendship founded in slavery, still exists today. In Gee's Bend, Alabama, you will find a group of women who are direct descendants of enslaved people. These friends are the most skillful quilters you ever will meet. Generations of women in Gee's Bend have gathered to make quilts. This ritual has helped them through hard times, depression, racism, the civil rights movement, and tragedy. In the '60s, their talent caught the attention of Martin Luther King Jr., who stopped there on his way to Selma. In 2018, Amy Sherald, the artist who painted First Lady Michelle Obama's official portrait, also visited the town. You can see the influence of the quilts in her painting. Ms. Sherald said the quilts pay homage to the African-American heritage.

The award-winning quilts also have been on display in museums all over the country. Through their talent, the women of Gee's Bend have celebrated friendship while preserving history and tradition with needle and thread. Together, these friends not only kept their families warm but also provided an income that put food on their tables (Ronan, 2018). Each stitch is a tribute to their lives, friendship and heritage. Every square represents stories, tears, dedication, heartache, joy and laughter. I wonder if the enslaved quiltmakers of the 1800s understood they would provide skills and income for their descendants two centuries later? Although these quilts did not bring their creators wealth in a monetary sense, they brought abundance, joy, service and connection — all of which happen when women come together.

Stepping back into 1821 in Philadelphia, we will find a group of friends who formed The Daughters of Africa Society. These free Black women transformed their friendship into a service for others. They offered financial aid and support to people in their community, while encouraging each other to pursue their dreams. Their friendship helped Black people to find jobs during a time when they had few to no opportunities to make money. This group enabled many people of color to live lives they otherwise would not have been able to experience (Yalom and Brown, 2015).

A female friendship established in the mid-1800s brought about a change to the U.S. Constitution. Susan B. Anthony and Elizabeth Cady Stanton are the foremothers of the 19th Amendment, which guarantees women the right to vote. The two women met in 1851 at an anti-slavery rally and became instant friends. They shared a vision of equality for women. Using each other's strengths — Elizabeth's ability to inspire and Susan's ability to organize — they published a newspaper, held protests and rallies, and started the national suffrage movement. Although these two friends did not live to see the ratification of the 19th Amendment, they are credited for paving the way. (Historical documentation suggests that the women did not fight hard enough for Black and Brown women to be seen as equal citizens. I believe the adage is true: Until all women are equal, no woman is equal.)

In the late 1800s and early 1900s, colleges and universities started accepting women into their schools. As attendance grew, so did friendships. Women relied on each other for tutoring. They ate meals together, roomed together and attended extracurricular activities. Receiving an education while having the freedom to be with friends was a new experience. Being with those who provide you with a sense of belonging is good for the soul.

For young women who entered the workforce, friendships meant independence. In the 1900s, it was uncommon for a girl to move out of her parents' home and live on her own. However, coworkers who became trusted friends could share rent, groceries and utility bills. Finding a special friend who was trustworthy enough to live and work with meant freedom for young women of all races.

Across the world in Egypt, women were coming together to fight for equality and end oppression. Between 1892 and 1920, women in Egypt were sharing literature, progressive thoughts and art — all in attempts to affirm and improve women's lives in Arab nations. Three women, in particular, partnered together to advance the cause. Huda Sha'arawi, Malak Hifni Nasif, and Nabawiyya Musa worked to improve women's health care, gain educational opportunities and give women a voice in a nation that had yet to recognize them as full citizens. These women were founding mothers of the feminist movement in Egypt. Their ability to partner together gave other women strength when they were considered powerless (Badawey, 2016).

Women seem to have an innate ability to know when people need to be lifted. As women worldwide united in the fight for equality, they also came together to serve those in need. Friends realized the power and resources they possessed could help their fellow citizens, so it should be no surprise that female friends started many nonprofits and wartime efforts. While most friendship groups were based on social class, the organizations born from these friendships reached across economic status and race.

During World War I, friends organized volunteer opportunities to collect items needed to support the soldiers abroad. These opportunities offered all women the chance to become a united force to support the wartime efforts. They understood their ability to rally and inspire others. When women come together, it benefits the whole community. Through friendships, they started homes for displaced families, orphanages, soup kitchens and schools. They fought for the underprivileged just as much as they fought for themselves.

When women come into a relationship, they bring empowerment. The women's movement picked up steam in the late '60s and early '70s. Women in the workplace faced opposition. They weren't considered for raises or promotions and could even be fired for being pregnant. Actor Marlo Thomas and activist Gloria Steinem formed a friendship entrenched in making lives better for other women. They spoke out against discrimination in the workplace. When businesses were reluctant to hire women because they might become pregnant, Gloria and Marlo protested. When single mothers needed childcare and better healthcare, Gloria and Marlo rallied to support them. Together, the duo — along with Letty Cottin Pogrebin and Marie C. Wilson — started the Ms. Foundation for Women, a nonprofit focused on supporting women-led initiatives that advocate equality, focusing on minorities. Gloria and Marlo held each other accountable to be the best versions of themselves and fight for all women's rights.

In 2014, a group of 10 friends dared to do the impossible: They formed the first all-female Afghan Orchestra. But, first, let me give you some background. Twice a terrorist group called the Taliban has taken control of Afghanistan and enforced very strict religious laws. One of their many oppressive rulings was a ban on music. Even more upsetting, they also took all rights away from women. So, no music and no rights for women.

However, in 2014, one brave young trumpet player, Meena — along with her friends at Afghanistan's National Institute of Music — had an idea. Meena approached a faculty member and asked if she and her friends could form the country's first all-female orchestra. Suggesting that a group of young women rise up and play music in a country where it is banned is a harmonious act of courage. The Institute supported the friends' request, and they started the symphony. Today, it is 30 members strong. They travel the world and entertain millions of people (Ensemble Zohra Afghan's Women Orchestra, n.d.). After the second time the Taliban took over, the young women in the orchestra attempted to leave the country; sadly, only a few managed to escape (Raghavan, 2021). Every note they play enforces the idea that life should be filled with music and equality. This beautiful belief was started with 10 young friends, daring to be brave.

Girls, I am telling you that friendships feed our souls and make the world better. There is nothing like a friend who pushes you to dare greatly and chase your passions.

## She Feels Like Home
Understanding What Makes a Good Friend

Friends enrich our lives. They make the sweet parts better and the complex parts bearable. When I established my business, it was with the help of some of the dearest women in my life. I knew their hearts, strength, determination and wisdom. I wanted to be surrounded by it and soak up a little for myself. There was no way I could have done what I did without those women. I am forever grateful for them.

What I want you to understand is that friendships are about the lift. If you aren't receiving that from a friend, sweet girl, she is not a friend. Some people are just meant to be acquaintances — people you are friendly with, but not those you trust with your heart. There also are those you think will be your lifelong friends, and it just doesn't turn out that way. Someone gets hurt, someone walks away, someone outgrows the relationship. These things are okay. This is a part of life that everyone goes through. In fact, it is in navigating these challenging experiences that you learn the most about yourself. Relationship struggles allow you to reflect on who you are and what you want from life. Then, when you can find the people who want similar things, bonds will form.

*Sweet Girls,*

*The truth about friendships is that they are filled with ups and downs. It is impossible to get along with everyone every minute of the day and it's just as impossible to not get annoyed by others. But, once you find the person you can trust enough to disagree with, you have found the girl you can trust enough to be a friend. If you don't feel a relationship can last through a disagreement, then it's too fragile for a true friendship. Find the girls who want to get into the trenches of life with you. Find the girls who want to talk about silly fashion trends, help you fix your hair for prom, tell you when your makeup is too much, hold you when life is hard, keep you in check when you are being dramatic, and help you get something unstuck from your teeth. Look for friends who urge you to step out of shame when you make a mistake. Stick with the girls who tell you when you are wrong and back you up when you are right. Don't settle and never force a friendship. Listen to that small voice inside of you. If your spirit says "no," keep walking and continue looking for her. She is out there looking for you. You will know when you find her. There will be a peaceful settling in your heart.*

*She will feel like home.*

The girls who will be your friends are the ones who don't care how different you are. They care about how much you support them, laugh with them and empathize with them. You will want the same from them. Friendships never are about fitting in. They are about belonging. "Fitting in" says everything has to be the same. "Belonging" means that differences are celebrated just as much as similarities.

When forming friendships with other girls, remember:
• Look for people who accept the real you.
• Never change who you are to fit in with others.
• Be friends with girls who want to support you and whom you want to support.
• Hang around people who make you feel comfortable.
• You were made to belong.
• Relationships made through social media are not the same as friendships.
• "Likes" on social-media posts are not a reflection of one's likeability.

Parents,

Guiding your daughter through friendship woes is an emotional experience. My daughter had a group of close acquaintances throughout school, but she didn't find her friends until the end of high school. The life lessons that come from relationships are some of the most prickly and painful experiences. Being left out and feeling lonely or "less than" are lessons we learn from people. Sometimes we misuse people's hearts, and there are times people hurt ours. Working through your daughter's tears when she has been left off the invitation list is almost unbearable. Telling her she isn't less because they did not invite her seems like a futile conversation to have. No amount of parenting or guidance will prevent this type of pain. The good news is that these experiences are where resilience grows, grit is formed, grace is birthed, and self-love starts. If my mother said it to me once, she said it a thousand times: "This too shall pass." And it did.

Parents, you and I have lived through all of our worst days, and your daughter will make it through hers as well. Eventually, she will heal and find her person to call, laugh and hang out with. Teaching her to know and trust herself also will help her understand what she wants out of her friendships. She will see that not being invited to the party was okay because those obviously weren't her people. This conversation can be a befuddling one. Go with your gut, love and grace. If you make a wrong move, apologize. Tell her this is new territory for you, and she will understand.

When guiding your daughter through friendships, here are some important things think about:

- Fitting In versus Belonging.
- Not being included does not make you less than.
- How meaningful are your (the parents') friendships?
- Does your daughter have the ability to contact her friends when she is not at school?
- What interpersonal skills does your daughter have, and what needs to be developed?
- Work with your daughter to have a mental script of things to say when friendships feel sticky or problematic.
- Work with your daughter to have a mental script of things to say to someone with whom she is interested in developing a friendship.
- As hard as it is to see your kiddos in pain, remember that these are the spaces where life lessons happen and confidence grows.
- Fight against the negative stereotypes of female friendships. Girls are not always gossips.
- Drama and gossip are born out of jealousy and self-doubt. When we teach our daughters to be authentic in their relationships, they become confident. Jealousy and self-doubt cannot thrive in confidence.
- Consider how much you gossip with your friends.

- Discuss the importance of boundaries in relationships: when to not tell secrets, what to do when someone expects too much from your daughter or when she expects too much from others.
- Discuss how relationships on social media are not the same as real-life friendships.
- "Likes" on social media mean absolutely nothing when it comes to true friendships or your daughter's likeability.
- If you are like me and have a son or daughter, talk to them both about friendships and let them see how to wisely navigate one of life's most precious gifts.

## Giggles & Late-Night Conversations
10 Fun & Slightly Crazy Facts About Friendships

- Some species of animals can form friendships.
- Friendships improve your health.
- Our brains react the same way when our friends or we are in trouble.
- It's scientifically proven that friends reduce stress.
- Friendships are more robust when you know what irritates each other.
- Most people have 3-5 close friends.
- On average, people make 396 friends during a lifetime.
- Babies as young as 9 months understand friendships.
- Marriages rooted in friendships last longer than those that aren't.
- The closest friends have a similar genetic makeup.

*You are enough.*

*You.*
*Are.*
*Enough.*

You Are Enough

# CONCLUSION

◆———◆———◆

Enough:
Sufficient for the need.

What I've learned:
You are enough.

*Sweet Girls,*

*We have come to the end of our conversation. It was my intention to take you on a quick journey through time to visit the origins of beauty culture. I wanted to help you understand why people believe what they do about beauty culture and how it affects girls. I tried to crack open the hard shell of judgment and silence. I attempted to explain the forgotten history, hoping to release any shame surrounding the feminine body. I wanted to stop doubt before it made its way to you. I hope I achieved this and empowered you to take charge of your body.*

*Here's the thing. You already are stunning, every bit of you. There is absolutely nothing you have to do to make yourself beautiful; it's already there. You are beauty, and beauty is you! The only thing you need to do is breathe it all in. All of your stunning loveliness, all of your talent, all of your you-ness. Breathe it in and make it your truth.*

*You were made for you. To dream big and set goals specific to and for yourself, not for anyone else. Your body was made just for you — for you to love and to be proud of, to express yourself and to care for. Shame has no claim on your body. You have everything you need to break free from beauty routines and beliefs that hurt you. You have the power to say "no" to anything that takes self-love away from you. Use that power, say that word, and then keep walking. "No" is guilt-free and "no" is a complete sentence.*

*My great-grandfather was German. He was known for saying, "Wir leben nur einmal," which translates to, "We only live once." You have this one life and this one body — so don't waste years wishing you were thinner, prettier, taller, shorter or bigger.*

*Love your body now.*

*Understand that it is enough now.*

*If I could give you anything, it would be self-love. A gentle love that walks its own path passes by self-doubt and pretend beauty. It detours around other people's opinions and heads straight toward authenticity. You are in charge. You have the power not only to determine your future but also to create your own herstory. Do it with grace. Do it with your own style and flair. Do it with makeup, shaved legs and dreadlocks. Or do it with a natural face, hairy legs and spiky pink hair. Just be yourself and honor your spirit. It will get awkward, but remember: It's all figure-outable.*

*Always be unapologetically you because you are enough.*

*You are enough.*

*You.*
*Are.*
*Enough.*

Always,

## ACKNOWLEDGMENTS

This book expresses the love between one generation and another. From a mother to a daughter. From an aunt to her niece. From grandmother to granddaughter. From a woman to her body.

TO EVERY GRACEFULLY STRONG GIRL & THE WOMEN WHO GAVE IT FLIGHT:
Girls, you are the reason I am writing this book. You are my passion and you will change the world. Love yourselves and fly high. I believe in you.

TO MY CHILDREN, IZZY & RAFE:
You understood when my door was shut and my mind was too full of words. I love you and am so proud of who you are and how you are living your lives. May you both know how to use the word "no" without guilt, grow to be independent, wise and full of grace. You impress me every day. Rafe, thank you for understanding why girls need this book and for embracing feminism; you are among the wisest of men. Izzy, thank you for being my girl, for shaping me into the woman I am today. Your grace is a balm. I got a lot of it wrong but, together, we got so much of it right.

MAGGIE THE CUPCAKE:
Never lose your sense of fashion. You are enough. Always have been, always will be.

MADDOX:
Never stop being curious and tap away.

SHANE:
Thanks for raising feminists; you are changing the world.

SHELLA:
Thank you for your passion, enthusiasm and support. You always are one of my biggest cheerleaders and fiercest allies. Thanks for reminding me about the two Vs. Be a good neighbor and stay on the journey, sister — all my love always.

DADA:

Thank you for your calm, consistent love and support. You lived with three women who all had the most stubborn ways because we saw things differently than those around us. You respected this and raised feminists. Thank you. You are my rock and the wisest among men.

MOM:

Where to start? Thanks for letting me write about you. Thanks for seeing the humor, for your devotion to my journey, and for proofing every bit of this book. You taught me to be my own best friend. You are eternal.

TO MY AUNTS & UNCLES:

You always were there, investing in me — and thereby showing me that I was enough. My aunts, you are warrior women.

MY COUSINS, WHO ARE CHANGING CONVERSATIONS:

You were my first friends, along with being the source of my loudest laughs and greatest delights. Let us never stray from each other.

GRANNY, GRAMPS & GRANDMA:

You laid a foundation. You are the joy that comes in the morning.

MEAGAN & THE ERIN:

You kept (and keep) me organized so I could work on my passion. I treasure and appreciate you both.

BEN:

Thank you for your creativity.

KIM:

Thank you for the polish and shine.

ANGELA & ABUZZ:
My thanks to you for taking a chance on this novice writer and believing this
book was worthy of going to press.

ANNI:
Thank you for capturing the spirit of our mission.

BRANDON:
You simply have no idea. From business partner to dearest friend, you are
a backbone and a foundation. The beauty of this book is because of you. Your
gifts and your talents are immense and you share them willingly. Thank you.

MK:
Your sweet support is a constant blessing.

TIMBS GIRLS:
Thank you for being my grounding force, my laughter, my Parrotheads,
my vault, my kitchen-table dose of reality, and also for riding my roller
coasters with me.

LISA:
Because of all the things too vast to mention, you are forever in my heart.

SHANNON:
You are the nurturing spirit I will forever love, especially the salty side
of you that is always on time when I need backup.

MAMO:
There will always be you.

PENNY PAIGE:
To my keeper of all the things, thank you for your encouragement, for all of the
hard conversations, the tears, the quirks, the laughs, the secrets, the journey,
the chats, the writing retreats, and for you. What would I do without you?

And, finally,

My Lanham:
This book is because of you. You pulled me aside,
said the words I needed to hear and, in doing so,
saved me. You are my soft place, my wisdom, my heart,
my breath, my love. We are so entwined I am not sure
where your soul stops and mine begins. Thank you for
believing in me, for your calm, your wisdom, your
unwavering support, and for always saying "Okay."
I love you.

F.A.A.D,
Bright Eyes

In 2015, Heather Stark stepped down from her role as a school counselor and started a girl-empowerment business called Grace & Grit. Stark has a Master of Education in School Counseling from Dallas Baptist University and a Bachelor of Arts in Psychology from The University of North Texas. She is the recipient of the 2018 Girls Scouts Women of Distinction Award and the 2019 recipient of the American Legion Humanitarian of the Year. Stark lives on Padre Island with her husband, children and two energetic dogs.

## BIBLIOGRAPHY

Boyce, S. (n.d.).
*History of Makeup in Egypt*
makeup.lovetoknow.com/History_of_Makeup_in_Egypt

Ancient Chinese Make Up (n.d.).
ancientchinafashion.weebly.com/make-up.html#:~:text=Especially%20in%20
the%20Tang%20Dynasty,%2C%20lastly%2C%20applied%20lip%20colour

OptionL2. (2013, June 5).
*Male Make-Up in Eighteenth Century England*
18centurybodies.wordpress.com/2013/06/05/male-make-up-in-eighteenth-
century-england

Brumberg, J. (1997).
*The Body Project: An Intimate History of American Girls*
NY, NY: Random House Inc.

A History of Cosmetics from Ancient Times (2016).
cosmeticsinfo.org/get-the-facts/a-history-of-cosmetics-from-ancient-times

Nittle, N. (2018, Jan. 23).
*Before Fenty: Over 100 Years of Black Makeup Brands*
racked.com/2018/1/23/16901594/black-makeup-brands-history

Booth, J. (2019, April, 23).
*17 Incredibly Disturbing Beauty Trends From History*
itsblossom.com/most-disturbing-beauty-trends

Zarias. (n.d.).
30 Interesting Facts about Makeup and Cosmetics
zarias.com/30-interesting-facts-makeup-cosmetics

Nesvig, K. (2015, Feb. 16).
*25 Little-Known Facts About Makeup*
thoughtcatalog.com/kara-nesvig/2015/02/25-little-known-facts-about-makeup

Biography.com Editors. (2016, April 5).
Elizabeth Arden Biography
biography.com/business-figure/elizabeth-arden

The Editors of Encyclopedia Britannica. (n.d.).
Eunice Walker Johnson. American Entrepreneur.
www.britannica.com/biography/Eunice-Walker-Johnson

Knight, E. (20018, March 10).
*Historical Methods of Hair Removal*
https://www.historyundressed.com/search?q=ladies-have-you-ever-forgotten-to-shave

Ancient Man and His First Civilizations (n.d.).
realhistoryww.com/world_history/ancient/Egypt_1a.htm

The History of Sugaring (2016, March 2).
puresugarhb.com/blog/2016/1/26/the-history-of-sugaring

McKay, B. and McKay, K. (2012, June 7).
*Unique Shaving & Grooming Rituals from History and Around the World*
artofmanliness.com/articles/shaving-rituals/

Cosmetics and Personal Care Products in the Medicine and
Science Collections: Hair Removal (n.d.).
si.edu/spotlight/health-hygiene-and-beauty/hair-removal

Women's Museum of California. (2017, Nov. 22).
Beauty or Torture: The History of Female Hair Removal
womensmuseum.wordpress.com/2017/11/22/the-history-of-female-hair-removal

Gooley, G. (2018, July 12).
*How the Founder of Billie Razors Is Disrupting the Male-Dominated Shaving Industry*
time.com/5336199/billie-founder-disrupt-shaving-industry

Elliott, C. (2019).
*The Pink Tax: The Cost of Being a Female Consumer*
listenmoneymatters.com/the-pink-tax

Building a future for women (2019).
mybillie.com

*The History and Culture of 'Black Hair'* (n.d.).
afrotexturedhistory.tumblr.com/post/79889148950/the-african-context-of-hair-
in-ancient-egypt

Ancient Egyptian Hair And Beauty (n.d.).
purchasereq.tripod.com/id9.html

Ahmose-Nefertari (n.d.).
wikiwand.com/en/Ahmose-Nefertari

The Hair in Ancient Times (n.d.).
thehistoryofthehairsworld.com/old_age_2.html

Astral, N. (n.d.).
*the Science of ancient Egyptian hair and why it sometimes looks European*
https://sites.google.com/site/naomiastral/ancient-kemet/the-science-of-ancient-
egyptian-hair

James, J. (2017, Oct. 6).
*The Unheard of History of the Hairdresser*
owlcation.com/humanities/HairdresserHistory

Zhan, J. (2015, May 10).
*Ancient Lifehack: Haute Coiffure — Fashion Dos & Don'ts*
shenyunperformingarts.org/blog/view/article/e/QfDb-EMLzYk/asian-hairstyles-lifehack-ancient-chinese-haute-coiffure

YABAI Writers. (n.d.).
The Importance of Hairstyles for the Japanese
yabai.com/p/2890

The Hair in the Middle Ages (n.d.).
thehistoryofthehairsworld.com/middle_ages_renaissance.html

The hair at the Eighteenth century (n.d.).
thehistoryofthehairsworld.com/hair_18th_century.html

Shaw, S. (2019, Nov. 1).
*How Marie Antoinette's Hair was a Harbinger for the French Revolution*
https://crfashionbook.com/culture-a29655776-marie-antoinette-hair-leonard-autie/

Hopp, D. (2019, Oct. 04).
*From 1500 BC to 2015 AD: The Extraordinary History of Hair Color*
byrdie.com/hair-color-history

The Significance of Hair in Native American Culture (2019, Jan. 4).
sistersky.com/blogs/sister-sky/the-significance-of-hair-in-native-american-culture

Lightening Woman Johnstone, P. (1998, Sept. 4).
*Hair Raising... A Spiritual Journey*
https://www.keepersoftheword.org/traditions/native-americans-long-hair/

Booker, K. (2014, Feb. 21).
*A History Of Black Hair In America*
refinery29.com/en-us/black-hair-history#slide-26

Jahangir, R. (2015, May 31).
*How does black hair reflect black history?*
bbc.com/news/uk-england-merseyside-31438273

Sessions, D. (2018, June 5).
*1950s Hairstyles – 50s Hairstyles from Short to Long*
https://vintagedancer.com/1950s/1950s-hairstyles/

Ridder, M. (2020, Nov. 23).
*Size of the global hair care market from 2012 to 2025 (in billion U.S. dollars)**
statista.com/statistics/254608/global-hair-care-market-size/#statisticContainer

Foussianes, C. (2020, March 22).
*Did* Self-Made *Base Madam C.J. Walker's Rival, Addie Monroe, on Annie Malone?*
townandcountrymag.com/society/tradition/a31751797/self-made-madam-cj-walker-
annie-turnbo-malone-rival-true-story

Mejia, N. (2020, Sept. 18).
*'How I Went From Hating My Natural Hair To Starting A Proudly Afro-Latina
Haircare Brand'*
womenshealthmag.com/beauty/a33984391/ada-rojas-botanika-beauty

Michalska, M. (2020, Oct. 17).
*Ancient Bikini Girls from the Roman Mosaics*
https://www.dailyartmagazine.com/ancient-bikini-girls

Corset History (n.d.).
champagnecorsets.com/history

Nhean, C. (2016, Mar. 30).
*From Bombs to Bras: World War I Conservation Measures Transform
the Lives of Women*
https://connecticuthistory.org/from-bombs-to-bras-world-war-i-conservation-
measures-transform-the-lives-of-women/

Crandall, D. (2018, April 26).
*100 Years of Brassieres: The Historical Evolution of the Bra*
insidehook.com/article/history/100-years-brassieres-inside-historical-evolution-bra

Maidenform, Inc. History (n.d.).
fundinguniverse.com/company-histories/maidenform-inc-history

Swan, T. (2015).
*The Outlaw: Jane Russell's Breasts and Howard Hughes' Quest to Build a Better Bra*
https://hiddenremote.com/2014/08/05/outlaw-jane-russells-breasts-howard-hughes-quest-build-better-bra/

Bastone, K. (2017, Aug. 30).
*A Brief History of the Sports Bra*
https://www.runnersworld.com/runners-stories/a20860634/a-brief-history-of-the-sports-bra/

Monet, D. (2020, Jan. 19).
*History of Clothing: Why Do We Wear Clothes*
bellatory.com/fashion-industry/History-of-Clothing-Why-We-Wear-Clothes

Who invented clothes? A Palaeolithic archaeologist answers (n.d.).
https://www.theguardian.com/science/sifting-the-evidence/2013/may/20/who-invented-clothes-palaeolithic-archaeologist

S. Brown (2012).
*Fashion: The Definitive History of Costume and Style*
N.Y., N.Y.; DK Publishing

Egyptian Footwear (n.d).
fashionencyclopedia.com/fashion_costume_culture/The-Ancient-World-Egypt/Egyptian-Footwear.html

Women's Clothes in Ancient Rome (2018, Jan. 24).
owlcation.com/humanities/Womens-Clothes-in-Ancient-Rome

Ancient Chinese Clothing (n.d.).
ancientchinafashion.weebly.com

Foreman, A. (2015, February).
*Why Footbinding Persisted in China for a Millennium*
smithsonianmag.com/history/why-footbinding-persisted-china-millennium-
180953971

Gilbert, R. (n.d.).
*Medieval Clothing & Dress Accessories*
rosaliegilbert.com/clothesandaccessories.html

Sumptuary Laws of the Middle Ages (2017).
lordsandladies.org/sumptuary-laws-middle-ages.htm#:~:text=English%20
Sumptuary%20Laws%20were%20imposed,specific%20class%20structure%20
was%20maintained.

Munday, A. (2020, April 26)
*Medieval Shoes and Pattens*
aprilmunday.wordpress.com/2020/04/26/medieval-shoes-and-pattens

Wynne, E. (2017, Nov. 12).
*History of the high heel: It wasn't always a woman's shoe*
abc.net.au/news/2017-11-13/why-do-we-wear-high-heeled-shoes/9135936

McNamara, K. (2017, March 24).
*Panniers*
https://fashionhistory.fitnyc.edu/panniers/

Major Fashion Trends and Styles of the 1700s (n.d.).
mentalitch.com/major-fashion-trends-and-styles-of-the-1700s

Bellis, M. (2019, Jan. 7).
*History of the Sewing Machine*
thoughtco.com/stitches-the-history-of-sewing-machines-1992460

Monet, D. (2020, Jan. 1).
*Women's Clothing of the South in the American Civil War*
bellatory.com/fashion-industry/WomensClothingoftheSouthintheAmericanCivilWar

Green, J. (2012, April 1).
*Women's Fashion During the Civil War*
jocelyngreen.com/2012/04/01/womens-fashion-during-the-civil-war

(2017, Jan. 19).
The history of haute couture / From humble beginnings to present day
harpersbazaar.com/uk/fashion/fashion-news/news/a31123/the-history-of-
haute-couture/

Bae, Y. (n.d.).
*Clothing and Garment Manufacturing*
encyclopedia.chicagohistory.org/pages/300.html

Edwards, B. (n.d.).
*Department Store*
fashion-history.lovetoknow.com/fashion-clothing-industry/department-store

Robinson, K. (n.d).
The Origins of Clothing Sizes
seamwork.com/issues/2016/01/the-origins-of-clothing-sizes

Gerstein, J. (2014, April 2).
*71 Mind-Blowing Facts About The Clothes You're Wearing*
buzzfeed.com/juliegerstein/71-mind-blowing-facts-about-the-clothes-youre-wearing

Centeno, A. (n.d.).
*25 Random Fashion Facts You've NEVER Heard*
realmenrealstyle.com/random-fashion-facts

Mann, L.
*From Slavery to the White House: The Extraordinary Life of Elizabeth Keckly* (n.d.).
whitehousehistory.org/elizabeth-keckley

Phelps, N. (2019, Aug. 26).
*Designer Isabel Toledo Has Died*
vogue.com/article/isabel-toledo-obituary

Friedman, V. (2019, Aug. 26).
*Isabel Toledo Dies at 59; Designed Michelle Obama's Inaugural Outfit*
nytimes.com/2019/08/26/style/isabel-toledo-dead.html

Hrdy, S. (1999).
*Mother Nature: Maternal Instincts and How They Shape the Human Species*
New York, New York: The Ballantine Publishing Group.

Frandsen, P. (2007).
*The Menstrual "Taboo" in Ancient Egypt*
Journal of Near Eastern Studies, 66(2), 81-106. doi:10.1086/519030

Habiger, P. (1998).
*Early History: Menstruation, Mental Hygiene and Woman's Health in Ancient Egypt*
mum.org/germnt5.htm

schroeder, f. (1976).

*feminine hygiene, fashion and the emancipation of american women*

American Studies, 17(2), 101-110.

jstor.org/stable/40641221


Freidenfelds, L. (2017, Feb. 12)

*Period Drama: That Time of the Month in Victorian America*

civilwarmed.org/menstruating


Dupont, E. (2008, Sept. 30).

*Regnier de Graaf (1641-1673)*

https://embryo.asu.edu/pages/regnier-de-graaf-1641-1673


Gabillet, A. (2018, Oct. 1).

*What Did Women Do Before Tampons? A Brief History of Period Products*

bloodandmilk.com/brief-history-of-period-products


Mallasasime, B. (2021, July 8).

*Mary Kenner: The Inventor of Sanitary Belts*

historyofyesterday.com/mary-kenner-the-inventor-of-sanitary-belts-3fa94eb31d15


Yalom, M. and Donovan Brown, T. (2015).

*The Social Sex: A History of Female Friendship*

New York, New York: HarperCollins.


Cataneo, E. (2017, April 5).

*The Female Free Divers of Jeju*

roadsandkingdoms.com/2017/the-female-free-divers-of-jeju


The Editors of Encyclopaedia Britannica (2011, Oct. 20).

*Bluestocking*

britannica.com/topic/Bluestocking-British-literary-society